General Price-Level Accounting
Described and Illustrated

"People look for perfect solutions to every problem. Well there just aren't any perfect solutions for the problems of accounting. Never was one, never will be — now they are saying 'so you want to adjust by a price index. Well one index gives you 165; another 175; and still a third gives you 190. Since you can't say which index is best, we won't take any.' But surely the answer to that kind of comment is that you would be more nearly right if you used any one of the indexes than if you made no adjustment at all."

A Talk with George O. May.
Journal of Accountancy, June 1955

General Price-Level Accounting

Described and Illustrated

Alan D. Stickler, FCA *and*
Christina S. R. Hutchins, CA
Price Waterhouse & Co., Canada

The Canadian Institute of Chartered Accountants

DISCLAIMER

The Canadian Institute of Chartered Accountants has acted solely as publisher of this book. Neither it nor any provincial Institute or Order of Chartered Accountants, nor any Committee thereof, has officially reviewed this book, and hence do not assume any responsibility for its contents or for the use thereof.

Printed and bound in Canada

To the memory of
St. Elmo V. Smith, FCA,
a mentor and friend

Introduction

This book is intended to provide a practical guide to general price-level accounting and its purpose is to explain the methods and procedures used in this form of accounting. The book does not set out to argue the merits of general price-level accounting compared with, for example, those of replacement cost accounting as a solution to the general problem of accounting for inflation; nor does it discuss the arguments for or against retaining the historical cost basis. Those subjects have been and will, quite properly, continue to be discussed and it is perhaps not unreasonable to assume that from those discussions changes may emerge to replace eventually the historical cost basis. For the present, neither the business community nor the accountancy profession is ready to introduce current value accounting — in whatever form may eventually command general support; both however are seeking a means of providing the readers of financial statements with additional information about the effects of changes in the general purchasing power of money. The merits of general price-level accounting as a means to that end will continue to be debated. This book does not enter that debate but is written simply as a means of explaining the subject to those who may wish to apply general price-level accounting.

For this reason, we have attempted to discuss and illustrate the basic procedures for general price-level accounting and their application in as wide a variety of circumstances as possible. Because of the interest in the subject in Canada, the United Kingdom, the United States of America, and in many other parts of the world, we have endeavoured to discuss the subject in the light of these differing circumstances. Thus we have considered points which may have application only in some countries and do not have world-wide acceptance; in fact, some of the alternative historical cost accounting procedures discussed here in relation to general price-level accounting are not allowed by authoritative accounting standards or recommendations in some countries but are in common use in others.

The result of discussion and illustration on this scale may lead to an impression of complexity in the application of general price-level accounting. This impression is perhaps unfortunate because the adoption of general price-level accounting does not entail as immense an effort as a casual reading of this book might suggest. The extent of the effort required to introduce general price-level accounting will depend generally upon the amount of detail already available in the historical cost records. Furthermore, the effort required will undoubtedly be greatest in taking the preparatory steps; thereafter, general price-level statements can generally be completed without undue effort.

We recognize it is possible to develop short-cut approaches which will give an approximation of the results of applying general price-level accounting. Historical cost accounting already involves estimation and approximation. GPL accounting extends the limits of tolerance inherent in historical cost accounting. Without denying the possible uses of a short-cut approach as a means of approximating results by a rule of thumb method, we believe that an approximation method of GPL accounting would extend those limits of tolerance to an unacceptable degree for the purpose of providing information in annual reports. We have therefore confined ourselves to a theoretical and practical discussion of the procedures which would develop general price-level information of reasonable, though not absolute, precision.

General price-level accounting has been the subject of pronouncements for a number of years; present-day inflationary conditions have provided the impetus to bring its practical application to the fore in many countries. Consequently many of the problem areas in application have not yet been fully explored and are still under discussion or study by accountancy bodies. We have endeavoured to present the different viewpoints on the controversial issues which have yet to be resolved; in some cases it has been necessary to take one position or another on a given point for purposes of illustration. Nevertheless it has not been our task, and this book does not attempt, to anticipate the definitive standards or recommendations of any accountancy organization on general price-level accounting.

Alan D. Stickler
Christina S. R. Hutchins

Toronto, Canada
February, 1975

Table of Contents

Table of Exhibits

UNCONSOLIDATED STATEMENTS

CONSOLIDATED STATEMENTS

FOREIGN SUBSIDIARY STATEMENTS— UNITED KINGDOM

FOREIGN SUBSIDIARY STATEMENTS—SOUTH AMERICA

1

The Basics of General Price-Level Accounting

The purpose of general price-level accounting, or GPL accounting, is to isolate and measure the distorting effects of the change in the general purchasing power of currency during the period covered by a set of financial statements. This purpose is achieved by expressing all amounts in a constant unit of currency which is the purchasing power of the dollar at the date of those financial statements. Therefore GPL accounting involves the translation of amounts for transactions which took place at different times —and which were therefore recorded in dollars of different purchasing power—into dollars of the same purchasing power.

GPL accounting is normally thought of in relation to inflation, the decrease in the general purchasing power of currency. GPL accounting however is equally appropriate in relation to deflation, the increase in the general purchasing power of currency.

Basic to GPL accounting are:

- The adherence to generally accepted accounting principles.
- The use of a general price-level index.
- The application of conversion factors that are derived from that index.
- The distinction between monetary and non-monetary items in the financial statements.

Generally accepted accounting principles

GPL financial statements are based on the same accounting principles as historical financial statements. The numbers are changed because the unit of measurement is different, but the basic accounting concepts underlying the statements are not changed.

For example, if fixed assets are recorded in historical financial statements at an appraised value, the provision for depreciation is calculated by referring to that value and not to original cost. Similarly, when fixed assets are restated for purposes of GPL accounting, the provision for depreciation in the GPL income statement is calculated by referring to the restated amount. Or again, when the realization test is applied in historical statements and recognition is given to any impairment of the value of assets, the same test must be applied and, if necessary, any impairment recognized in the GPL statements. Possibly the application of the realization test could lead to a write-down in the GPL statements when none is required in the historical statements. Such a situation is illustrated in Chapter 4.

Price-level indices

Many countries publish different indices as matters of statistical record which measure changes in costs or prices. These indices can be considered in two main categories—general price-level indices and specific indices. General price-level indices are based on a relatively wide range of commodities and services which may be either typical of expenditures made by a cross-section of the population or indicative of the general effect of price changes on national expenditure accounts. Specific indices on the other hand relate as their name implies to particular goods or services of specific industries.

Because GPL accounting is intended to measure the effects of changes in the *general* purchasing power of currency, it is essential that a general price-level index be used to adjust historical cost statements, regardless of the particular industry within which a company operates.

There are many specific indices published by government bodies; these indices, by their nature, are not suitable for use in price-level accounting. Inflation is evidenced by changes in the general purchasing power of money, whereas specific indices measure only the value of money when it is related to or spent on specific things. To this extent, the use of a specific index will tend to reflect replacement cost and will not achieve the purpose of GPL accounting.

The use by a company of a specific price-level index may produce useful information for internal purposes in connection with, for example, its assets and inventories. But would the specific price-level index produce useful information in connection with items such as cash, receivables and debt? These items are related to the general purchasing power of money and only a general price-level index will produce relevant and useful information. Today many companies are conglomerates operating in different and widely varying industries; their consolidated fixed assets and inventories may be related to several different industries. One specific price index would therefore have little or no relevance to the consolidated assets. A general price-level index has equal relevance to all items in the financial statements. If it is assumed that all the various items in financial statements must be read together to present an overall picture of financial position and results of operations, it follows that the effects of a change in the value of money cannot be incorporated in those statements by using different indices to adjust different items, or by applying a given index to some items and making no adjustment at all to other items.

Conversion factors

Conversion factors are used to:

- translate the amount of transactions at the time they occurred to the equivalent of that same amount, measured in terms of purchasing power at the balance sheet date, and
- "roll forward" the figures from one balance sheet date to the next, that is, to update GPL financial statements to the equivalent in dollars of the same purchasing power at the next balance sheet date.

A conversion factor is calculated by dividing the purchasing power index of the dollar at the date of the balance sheet by the purchasing power index of the dollar at the date when a transaction occurred or at the date of the previous balance sheet which is to be rolled forward.

To illustrate this calculation, assume, for example, the use of the Canadian Consumer Price Index in which the indices are published as month-end figures and as annual averages. The monthly indices for 1973 were:

January	144.5	July	151.0
February	145.3	August	153.0
March	145.7	September	153.9
April	147.3	October	154.3
May	148.4	November	155.5
June	149.7	December	156.4

and the December 31 indices and annual averages from 1970 to 1973 were:

	December 31 index	*Annual average*
1970	129.8	129.7
1971	136.3	133.4
1972	143.3	139.8
1973	156.4	150.4

If a March 1973 transaction is to be translated into a number of dollars having the same purchasing power at December 1973, a conversion factor of 156.4/145.7, or 1.073 is applied to the amount of the transaction. Similarly, the conversion factor for a September 1973 transaction would be 156.4/153.9, or 1.016. Or, if a set of 1971 GPL statements is to be rolled forward to 1972 a conversion factor of 143.3/136.3, or 1.051 would be applied to each item in the 1971 statements. Similarly, the factor from 1972 to 1973 would be 156.4/143.3, or 1.091. In these cases the conversion factors have been expressed to three places of decimals. As a practical matter, this may often afford a sufficient degree of accuracy for GPL accounting, bearing in mind that the purpose is to measure a general and not a specific situation, but much will depend on the magnitude of the amounts involved and the extent to which they are rounded in the financial statements. In most situations however it is enough to express conversion factors to no more than three places of decimals.

Similarly, it may often be sufficient to select arbitrarily a starting point for GPL calculations. Share capital may have been issued or non-depreciable assets acquired a considerable number of years ago; there may be little practical merit but considerable practical difficulty in applying conversion factors for such transactions. The selection of an arbitrary date is a matter of judgement in the prevailing circumstances.

The use of monthly or average indices

Revenue and expense accrue evenly throughout the year in most businesses and it is therefore generally appropriate to use an average index when translating the income statement. For businesses which experience seasonal variations of trade, it may be advisable to translate revenue and expense according to monthly, quarterly or perhaps a weighted average index. Similarly for unusually large transactions it may be advisable to use the monthly or quarterly index.

In the case of the balance sheet when restating non-monetary items it is generally preferable to translate fixed assets and investments acquired during the current year at the actual index for the month or quarter in which the transaction occurred. However, when GPL accounting is first adopted it is necessary to translate such acquisitions made in prior years and for this purpose it is often adequate to use the average index of the year concerned.

If it is assumed that fixed asset expenditures had occurred evenly throughout each of the years 1970 to 1972 and in July 1973, the conversion factors to restate these expenditures in terms of December 31, 1973 purchasing power are calculated as follows, using the same indices as before.

1970	156.4/129.7, or 1.206
1971	156.4/133.4, or 1.172
1972	156.4/139.8, or 1.119

The numerator in each case is the index at December 31, 1973 and the denominator is the annual average index for the particular year.

1973	156.4/151.0, or 1.036

The numerator in this case is the index at December 31, 1973 and the denominator is the index for the month of July 1973.

So far as the conversion factors for use in restating the income statement are concerned, if it is assumed that the operations of the business have occurred fairly evenly throughout the year, a conversion factor based on the average index for the year would be calculated. Thus for 1973 the conversion factor would be 156.4/150.4, or 1.040. If the operations were of a seasonal nature and, for example, half of the sales were made during the first quarter of the year, the conversion factors for the sales of the first quarter would be:

$$156.4/(143.3 + 144.5 + 145.3 + 145.7) \div 4$$
or 156.4/144.7, or 1.081

and for the sales of the remaining three quarters would be:

$$156.4/(145.7 + 147.3 + 148.4 + 149.7 + 151.0 + 153.0 + 153.9 + 154.3 + 155.5 + 156.4) \div 10$$
or 156.4/151.5, or 1.032.

Distinction between monetary and non-monetary items

Apart from updating GPL statements from one year end to the next, conversion factors are applied only in the restatement of non-monetary items from dollars reflecting the purchasing power of money that prevailed when the various transactions occurred in the past to the number of dollars that would be required to provide the same purchasing power. Therefore, a clear distinction between monetary and non-monetary items is essential to the application of GPL accounting.

The classification of the majority of balance sheet items as monetary or non-monetary does not present a problem. However there are some items where the basis for classification is not clear-cut and these are discussed in Chapter 3.

Monetary items

Monetary items are defined as representing all items of which the amounts are fixed by contract or otherwise in terms of a specified number of dollars, regardless of changes in specific prices or in the general price-level of the dollar.

Monetary items include items such as cash, accounts and notes receivable, accounts and notes payable and debt payable in domestic currency. The fact that they are monetary items means they are already expressed in dollars which are equivalent to the general purchasing power of the dollar at a balance sheet date. Therefore, the monetary items are included in a GPL balance sheet at the same amounts at which they are stated in the historical cost balance sheet.

Non-monetary items

Non-monetary items are all items in the balance sheet (except the balance of retained earnings which is a residual) which cannot be classified as monetary and all items in the income statement. The non-monetary items in the balance sheet, such as fixed assets, are expressed in a mixture of dollars of different purchasing power, consisting perhaps of dollars of 1920 or 1950 or 1970 purchasing power. In GPL accounting all these dollars are translated into dollars of the same purchasing power.

The concept is similar to that used in translating foreign currencies. Australian dollars and South African rands are translated into their equivalents in Canadian dollars before being added in with Canadian dollars. Similarly a 1930 dollar and a 1970 dollar are translated into December 1974 dollars before being added in with other December 1974 dollars. The purpose of translating non-monetary items is to ensure that all items in the financial statements, both monetary and non-monetary, are expressed in their original purchasing power equivalents, using current dollars for this purpose.

There are some areas requiring special attention so far as non-monetary items are concerned which will also be discussed in Chapter 3.

2

Price-Level Gains and Losses

It has been explained that when historical cost financial statements are translated to GPL statements for any given period, monetary items at the end of the period remain the same and non-monetary items are adjusted in proportion to the inflation that has occurred since their acquisition. Although the monetary items are not restated at the balance sheet date, they are included in the general updating that occurs when all items in comparative statements are rolled forward to the end of the next year or accounting period; for example, at December 31, 1973 monetary items would not be restated but when the 1973 statements are rolled forward for use as comparative figures at December 31, 1974 they would be included in that general updating. This permits the calculation of the general price-level gain or loss, which is the result of holding monetary items during a period when the purchasing power of money is changing. Or in other words, the result of applying GPL accounting is that the effect of inflation on the monetary assets and liabilities is recognized currently in each accounting period as a general price-level gain or loss.

Non-monetary items do not gain or lose general purchasing power merely as a result of the changing value of the currency; the influence of the changing value of the currency on non-monetary items is combined with the changes in the specific prices of non-monetary items, which are due to many other factors such as changing technology and the laws of supply and demand in the market place. The restatement of non-monetary items to dollars of the same purchasing power does not result in the recognition *at that time* of any gain or loss in the income statement. Any gains or losses resulting from holding non-monetary items are recognized at the same time as they are recognized in the historical cost financial statements.

Calculation of the price-level gain or loss

> "General price-level gains and losses on monetary items . . . should be calculated by restating the opening balances and transactions in the accounts for monetary assets and liabilities to dollars of general purchasing power at the end of the period and comparing the resulting restated balances at the end of the period with the actual balances at the end of the period."[1]

A convenient method of making this calculation is to prepare a statement of source and application of monetary items in two columns, one for the historical cost amounts and the other for the historical cost amounts as restated into dollars of equivalent purchasing power at the closing balance sheet date. The statement might be drawn up as shown in Figure 2.1.

Statements of source and application of monetary items are included in the examples which follow in later chapters. These examples do not include statements of source and application of funds or changes in financial position although these statements

---

[1] Accounting Principles Board Statement No. 3, paragraph 40.

Figure 2.1

	Historical cost	*Restated to dollars of equivalent purchasing power at closing balance sheet date*
Net monetary items at opening balance sheet date	$	$
Add:		
Items resulting in monetary inflow		
Sales		
Proceeds from sale of assets		
Investment income	________	________
Deduct:		
Items resulting in monetary outflow		
Purchases		
Other expenses		
Interest		
Taxes		
Purchases of assets etc.		
Dividends	________	________
Net monetary items at closing balance sheet date		
Actual net monetary items on hand in closing balance sheet	________	________
Balance, i.e. gain or loss on holding monetary items		$________

are now a common feature of historical financial statements. In GPL accounting the funds statement serves no useful purpose; the statement of source and application of net monetary items provides most of the information normally included in a historical funds statement and is more relevant to GPL accounting.

Treatment of the price-level gain or loss

There are several schools of thought on how price-level gains or losses should be recognized.

1. All price-level gains or losses, regardless of source, should be recognized in the GPL income statement.
2. Price-level losses but not price-level gains should be recognized in the GPL income statement.
3. All price-level gains or losses should be recognized in the GPL income statement, except for that part of the gain or loss arising from long-term debt which should be deferred in the balance sheet.
4. All price-level gains or losses should be recognized in the GPL income statement, except for that part of the gain or loss arising from monetary items included in shareholders' equity, for example preferred shares having monetary characteristics.

The treatment of the price-level gain or loss has been argued in many books and articles; authoritative views on the subject are contained in the pronouncements of the various accountancy bodies. The main viewpoints were expressed in 1969 in APB Statement No. 3 of the American Institute of Certified Public Accountants.

> "41. General price-level gains and losses on monetary items arise from changes in the general price-level, and are not related to subsequent events such as the receipt or payment of money. Consequently, the Board has concluded that these gains and losses should be recognized as part of the net income of the period in which the general price-level changes.
>
> "42. A different viewpoint than that expressed in paragraph 41, held by a Board member, is that all of a monetary gain should not be recognized in the period of general price-level increase. Under this view, a portion of the gain on net monetary liabilities in a period of general price-level increase should be deferred to future periods as a reduction of the cost of non-monetary assets, since the liabilities represent a source of funds for the financing of these assets. The proponent of this view believes that the gain from holding net monetary liabilities during inflation is not realized until the assets acquired from the funds borrowed are sold or consumed in operations. The Board does not agree with this view, however, because it believes that the gain accrues during the period of the general price-level increase and is unrelated to the cost of non-monetary assets."

The conclusion reached by the APB that general price-level gains or losses be recognized in the GPL income statement has been sustained by the Financial Accounting Standards Board in its exposure draft issued December 1974, except for the gain or loss arising from monetary items included in shareholders' equity (see page 14 for further discussion). The following are relevant extracts from the exposure draft.

> "48. The net gain or loss of general purchasing power that results from holding monetary assets and liabilities shall be included in determining net income in units of general purchasing power. No portion of the general purchasing power gain or loss shall be deferred to future periods."

> "77. General purchasing power gains and losses on monetary assets and liabilities arise from changes in the general price-level while the assets are held or the liabilities are owed. They are not related to subsequent events such as the receipt or payment of money. Consequently, the Board concluded (paragraph 48) that those gains and losses should be recognized in determining general purchasing power net income in the period in which the general price-level changes."

This approach has also been followed by the Accounting Standards Steering Committee in the United Kingdom which published a Provisional Statement of Standard Accounting Practice No. 7 in May 1974.

> "16. It has been argued that the gain on long-term borrowing should not be shown as profit in the supplementary statement because it might not be possible to distribute it without raising additional finance. This argument, however, confuses the measurement of profitability with the measurement of liquidity. Even in the absence of inflation, the whole of a company's profit may not be distributable without raising additional finance, for example because it has been invested in, or earmarked for investment in, nonliquid assets.

> "17. Moreover, it is inconsistent to exclude such gains when profit has been debited with the cost of borrowing (which must be

assumed to reflect anticipation of inflation by the lender during the currency of the loan), and with depreciation on the converted cost of fixed assets."

Two points are made by the ASSC. One is that arguments against the recognition of price-level gains on long-term debt are confusing profitability with liquidity. In the historical cost statements, the amount shown as net income is not a measurement of liquidity; it may well include amounts which are not realized in cash although very properly included as income. Such amounts could result from instalment sales or other long-term sales where income is recognized currently although cash is not received currently. The fact that the price-level gain on long-term debt has not been realized is not in itself sufficient reason for excluding it from the GPL income statement.

The other point deals with matching the price-level gain on long-term debt against the cost of borrowing. In addition to this general aspect of matching, a further point to consider is when the debt has been incurred to finance specific fixed asset additions. Then, the inclusion of the price-level gain in income is logical to achieve a fairer matching with the increased depreciation which results when the fixed assets are restated.

The weight of authoritative accounting opinion thus supports the view that all price-level gains and losses should be recognized in the year in which they occur. This view is both logical and consistent with the basic theory of GPL accounting. The purpose of GPL accounting is to isolate and account for the effect on an enterprise of the general change in the purchasing power of money.

The price-level gain resulting from long-term debt is as much a part of the effect of inflation during the period as the price-level loss resulting from holding long-term bank or other deposits.

As a general rule all price-level gains or losses are recognized in the GPL income statement. An exception occurs in the case of gains or losses arising from monetary items included in shareholders' equity. Practice varies in different countries; in cases where gains or losses which arise from transactions with a company's own shareholders are not recognized in a historical cost income statement, they should not be included in the GPL income statement. In this connection, the FASB exposure draft recommends that gains or losses attributable to preferred shares carried at an amount equal to their fixed redemption or liquidation price should be credited or charged direct to shareholders' equity in the GPL balance sheet. Although not specifically recommended by the FASB it would be desirable that such gains should be credited to a separate account in the shareholders' equity section; losses would be charged so far as possible to the same account and thereafter to retained earnings.

It is important to remember that any price-level gain is not a realized gain in the sense that it is not represented by cash or other current assets. To avoid any possible misunderstanding by readers of GPL statements, it is advisable to explain in the financial statements how the gain arose and to emphasize that it is not represented by cash. Some enterprises have made this point quite clear in their financial statements, for example:

> *Institute of Chartered Accountants in England and Wales*
> "Gain on holding net monetary liabilities. The gain on holding net monetary liabilities is made up of £118,000 on the development loan and £23,000 on other items including the overdraft. It must, however, be stressed that whilst this is a real gain to members it is not represented by cash and could not, for example, be used to reduce subscriptions."

In thinking of price-level gains and losses arising from holding monetary items it is important to remember that these gains and losses are reported only for the period covered by the first income statement prepared on a GPL basis and then in each subsequent period's income statement. Price-level gains and losses accrued prior to the date of the first preparation of GPL statements are not reported. Price-level gains on long-term debt are recognized from the date of the first preparation of GPL statements and not retroactively to the date when the long-term debt was issued.

In contrast, the restatement of non-monetary items is made retroactively to the original date of acquisition. The increase in the carrying value of items is adjusted through the restatement of opening retained earnings.

3

Monetary and Non-monetary Items—Some Problem Areas

Most balance sheet items can be readily classified as monetary or as non-monetary but in some cases the basis for classification is not clear-cut. Some assets and liabilities combine both monetary and non-monetary characteristics, in which case the surrounding circumstances must be examined to determine the predominant characteristic. In other cases, opposing viewpoints are held as to the classification of items as monetary or non-monetary.

Because the classification of an item can have a material influence on GPL statements, the problem areas which may be encountered will be considered here in detail. There are also some points requiring special consideration so far as non-monetary items are concerned.

Preferred shares

The problem revolves around the point whether the preferred shareholders' interest in the assets of an enterprise is limited to a fixed amount of dollars or should be considered as a permanent investment similar to the interest of the common shareholders.

APB Statement No. 3 suggested classifying preferred stock as non-monetary on the basis that the amount accounted for is the proceeds received when the shares were issued. The FASB exposure draft comments that "preferred stock carried at an amount equal to its fixed liquidation or redemption price is monetary because the claim of the preferred stockholders on the assets of the enterprise is in a fixed number of dollars; preferred stock carried at less than its fixed liquidation or redemption price is non-monetary but becomes monetary when restated to an amount equal to its fixed liquidation or redemption price". The exposure draft also contains a recommendation that "gains or losses of general purchasing power that result from monetary stockholders' equity items, for example, preferred stock that is carried . . . at . . . fixed liquidation or redemption price, shall be charged or credited directly to common stockholders' equity in the general purchasing power financial statements". (There is no comparable recommendation as to the treatment of the gain or loss in the recommendations of other accountancy bodies.) Another viewpoint is that preferred shares are similar to long-term debt and should be treated in a similar manner, i.e. classified as monetary, thus giving rise to a price-level gain in the income statement.

Reference has been made on page 12 to the possibility of different practices in the treatment of the price-level gain on preferred shares which are classified as monetary. If this price-level gain is credited direct to shareholders' equity, the classification of preferred shares as monetary or non-monetary is relatively unimportant because it would only affect the composition of items of shareholders' equity. On the other hand, if this price-level gain is credited in the GPL income statement, the monetary/non-monetary classification becomes important because the net income will be greater in each year in which the preferred shares are outstanding and the total of shareholders' equity will not be the same until the shares are redeemed.

To illustrate how GPL net income is affected, assume a company issued preferred shares in 1965, redeemable for $100,000. If the shares were classified as non-monetary, their carrying value in the 1974 GPL statements might be, say, $165,000 in terms of December 31, 1974 dollars. If the shares are redeemed on January 1, 1975, the cost to the company will be $100,000 in December 31, 1974 dollars and a GPL gain of $65,000 will arise. However, if the shares were classified as monetary from 1965 until 1974, their carrying value in the 1974 GPL statements would be $100,000 in terms of December 31, 1974 dollars. Price-level gains totalling $65,000 in terms of December 31, 1974 dollars would have been credited to GPL income statements over the years 1966 to 1974. When the shares are redeemed on January 1, 1975 the cost to the company is still $100,000 in December 31, 1974 dollars but no gain arises on the redemption.

When the price-level gain on preferred shares is credited to income, the solution to the problem of classification requires study of the features of each issue of preferred shares. In most circumstances, preferred shares have predominantly monetary characteristics, as is evident for example when they carry redeemable provisions, and should be classified as monetary. However, preferred shares which are convertible into common shares and, for example, are traded on their common share characteristics, are of a non-monetary nature.

Deferred income taxes

The subject of deferred tax accounting has been one of extreme controversy in historical cost accounting for many years; this controversy spills over into the consideration of GPL accounting for deferred income tax balances.

The original point at issue was that of tax allocation versus flow-through accounting. This may be taken as having been resolved when tax allocation was prescribed in those countries whose accountancy bodies issue pronouncements and recommendations.

Differences of opinion continue as to the method of applying tax allocation—the deferral method or the accrual method. In Canada and the United States the deferral method is required to be followed; in the United Kingdom an exposure draft issued in May 1973 proposed the use of the deferral method, but the accrual method was in use previously and appears to have been generally retained pending resolution of the exposure draft proposal.

The essential difference between the two methods however is that, under the accrual method, tax allocation credit balances are classified as liabilities whereas under the deferral method they are classified as deferred credits representing the savings that will be amortized to income in future periods as a reduction of taxation provisions. It follows that in GPL accounting the liability which arises under the accrual method is a monetary item, while the deferred credit which arises under the deferral method is a non-monetary item.

This distinction based on the underlying theory of tax allocation was followed by the AICPA in APB Statement No. 3 where deferred taxes and deferred charges for income taxes were classified as non-monetary items; a similar classification was retained by the FASB in its exposure draft. On the other hand, the CICA in its Accounting Guideline[1] has based the classification of deferred taxes on practical considerations and has recommended their treatment as monetary items.

What are the practical considerations which influence this classification? In periods of continuing inflation, the result of a non-monetary classification would be the deferral of price-level gains into the future; they would be reflected in GPL restated income when the deferred tax balances were drawn down. This might be acceptable or even appropriate if the general pattern were that the total tax allocation balance reversed regularly after only a few years, but this is the exception rather than the rule.

Deferred tax balances arise in large measure as the result of governmental fiscal policy which traditionally has provided the business community with incentives which give an effective reduction of taxes. The effect of these incentives is often that of an

[1] "Accounting for the Effects of Changes in the Purchasing Power of Money", issued December 1974.

indefinite postponement of income taxes while an enterprise remains in business. When deferred tax balances continue generally to increase with only sporadic or infrequent instances of drawdown, the result of a non-monetary classification for GPL purposes would be the continual restatement of those balances with only a decreasing probability—or complete improbability—of the price-level gain being eventually recognized. By contrast, a monetary classification will result in the price-level gain being recorded annually as inflation occurs, which may afford a more realistic appreciation of the circumstances.

There are also practical difficulties as well in implementing a non-monetary approach to deferred taxes. When deferred taxes result from timing differences between depreciation booked and depreciation claimed, restatement of the accumulated tax balance can be made only by reference to a detailed analysis of that balance, which as a practical matter may often be unavailable and difficult to reconstruct. Thus, *for each year* in which fixed assets, depreciated at different amounts for book and tax purposes, have been acquired it is necessary to tabulate the timing differences arising in the first and each subsequent year of those assets and to calculate their deferred tax effect to which the conversion factors can be applied.

The result of treating deferred taxes as monetary or non-monetary can be illustrated by a simple example of a company which, on a historical cost basis, has income before income taxes of $200 in each of the years 1974 to 1977. Although it may not be typical of the pattern of deferred tax accounting, this illustration assumes for convenience a single asset on which the total related deferred tax balance is reversed within the span of the illustration.

	1974	*1975*	*1976*	*1977*
Income before income taxes	$ 200	$ 200	$ 200	$ 200
Income tax expense				
Current	60	70	80	190
Deferred	40	30	20	(90)
	100	100	100	100
Net income for year	$ 100	$ 100	$ 100	$ 100

On the historical cost basis the accumulated deferred tax account at 1976 contained:

Timing differences arising in	1974	$40
	1975	30
	1976	20
		$90

1. Treatment of deferred income taxes as non-monetary.

	1974		*1975*		*1976*		*1977*	
	Historical	*Price-level*	*Historical*	*Price-level*	*Historical*	*Price-level*	*Historical*	*Price-level*
Income before income taxes	$200	$273	$200	$252	$200	$231	$200	$210
Income tax expense								
Current	60	82	70	88	80	92	190	199
Deferred	40	56	30	37	20	23	(90)	(116)
	100	138	100	125	100	115	100	83
Net income	$100	$135	$100	$127	$100	$116	$100	$127

All GPL adjusted columns are presented at their historical purchasing power equivalents, viewed in retrospect from December 31, 1977. The figures for the amounts of deferred taxes are obtained, assuming indices and conversion factors as shown below:

	Indices		*Conversion factors based on annual average indices*	*Conversion factors to restate into 1977 $*
	Average	*End of Year*		
1974	95	100	100/ 95, or 1.053	133/100, or 1.330
1975	105	110	110/105, or 1.048	133/110, or 1.209
1976	115	121	121/115, or 1.052	133/121, or 1.099
1977	127	133	133/127, or 1.047	133/133, or 1.000

	Historical deferred taxes				*End of year $*				*1977 $*
1974	40	×	1.053	=	42	×	1.330	=	56
1975	30	×	1.048	=	31	×	1.209	=	37
1976	20	×	1.052	=	21	×	1.099	=	23
	90								116

The 1977 income statement shows a reversal of deferred income taxes in the historical cost statements of $90 and the entire balance in the GPL adjusted balance sheet must also be reversed. This amounts to $116 expressed in 1977 dollars.

2. Treatment of deferred income taxes as monetary.

	1974		*1975*		*1976*		*1977*	
	His-torical	*Price-level*	*His-torical*	*Price-level*	*His-torical*	*Price-level*	*His-torical*	*Price-level*
Income before income taxes	$200	$273	$200	$252	$200	$231	$200	$210
Income tax expense								
Current	60	82	70	88	80	92	190	199
Deferred	40	56	30	37	20	23	(90)	(90)
	$100	$138	$100	$125	$100	$115	$100	$109
Net income before price-level gain	$100	$135	$100	$127	$100	$116	$100	$101
Price-level gain on deferred taxes		16		7		3		
Net income	$100	$151	$100	$134	$100	$119	$100	$101

All GPL adjusted columns are presented in 1977 dollars.

The 1977 income statement again shows a reversal of deferred income taxes in the historical cost statement of $90. In 1977 the entire balance in the GPL adjusted balance sheet must also be reversed. But in this case the balance in the deferred tax account is also $90; the deferred tax balance is monetary so in the GPL balance sheet it is shown at the same dollar amount as in the historical cost balance sheet. Because the deferred tax balance has been classified as monetary in the years 1974, 1975 and 1976, there is a price-level gain to be recognized from postponing payment of income taxes to a future year during a period of inflation.

The different effects of the two methods on the income statement can be summarized as follows:

	Historical	*Price-level*	
		Monetary	*Non-monetary*
Net Income			
1974	$100	$151	$135
1975	100	134	127
1976	100	119	116
1977	100	101	127
	$400	$505	$505

The effect of treating deferred taxes as monetary or non-monetary over the entire life of the deferred tax balance is identical but there are significant differences to the income statement during that time.

The authors believe deferred tax balances should be classified as monetary items for purposes of GPL accounting and have adopted this approach in the examples which follow. This does not represent a change in the application of accounting principles from those followed in the historical financial statements. It relates solely to the classification as between monetary and non-monetary items and does not affect the basis of calculation of the deferred tax balances.

It is clear however from the earlier references to differences between the pronouncements of national accountancy organizations that this matter has not yet been resolved to the point of uniformity. Furthermore, changes to these pronouncements may be made. As the International Accounting Standards Committee is studying the subject of GPL accounting, it may be assumed that its pronouncement in due course will deal with the matter of classification of deferred tax balances.

Foreign currency

There are two alternative viewpoints regarding foreign currency on hand, claims to foreign currency and amounts payable in foreign currency. One approach is to regard the foreign currency as a commodity, the price of which can fluctuate; the other approach is to regard foreign currency as being similar to domestic currency items. The AICPA in APB Statement No. 3 summarized these two opposing viewpoints.

"21. The fact that the market price of an item does not change over long periods of time does not in itself indicate that the item is monetary. Thus gold is non-monetary because its price can fluctuate. The fact that the price did not fluctuate for over 30 years does not make gold a monetary item. When general price-levels moved upward, the holder of gold lost general purchasing power because the price of his asset did not move as much as other prices, and not simply as a result of general price-level changes. Foreign currency, accounts receivable and payable in foreign currency, and similar items are also non-monetary. The price of foreign currency, that is, the foreign exchange rate, can change. Therefore, the holder of foreign currency items does not gain or lose general purchasing power simply as a result of general price-level changes. If the exchange rate does not change when the general price-level changes because of international controls or other factors, the price of foreign currency is rising or falling at a different rate than the general price-level. The effect on the holder is the joint result of a change in the structure of prices and a change in the general level of prices, and therefore the items are non-monetary. Even though foreign currency items are non-monetary, they may be stated at the current foreign exchange rate in general price-level financial statements. Under these circumstances they would be treated as non-monetary items carried at current market value.

"22. A different viewpoint than that expressed in paragraph 21, held by a few Board members, is that foreign currency, accounts receivable and payable in foreign currency, and similar foreign currency items are similar to domestic monetary items. Foreign currency items should therefore be stated directly at the current (closing) foreign exchange rate in the general price-level balance sheet. The effect on the income of the holder of foreign currency items is the joint result of both the change in the foreign exchange rate and the change in the domestic general price-level, and the items are therefore complex. Both effects are measurable, however, and should be disclosed separately. In the general price-level income statement, the effect of the general price-level change should be reported as a general price-level gain or loss on monetary items and the effect of the change in the exchange rate should be reported as a foreign exchange gain or loss. If the foreign exchange rate does not change, only a general price-level gain or loss should be reported."

The AICPA concluded that foreign currency, whether receivable or payable, should be classified as non-monetary. A similar classification has been made by the CICA in its Accounting Guideline. However, it is reasonable to suggest that when foreign currency items are translated in historical financial statements at the current rate of exchange, rather than at a historical rate of exchange, they should be classified as monetary items for GPL purposes.

Long-term debt in foreign currency

Long-term debt not payable in a foreign currency is classified as monetary in GPL statements, but in situations where the long-term debt is payable in a foreign currency the liability has both monetary and non-monetary characteristics. The question then arises as to whether the monetary or non-monetary aspect should prevail, and is particularly significant in Canada where there are numerous examples of long-term debt payable in a foreign currency.[1]

Although foreign currency was classified as a non-monetary item by the AICPA in APB Statement No. 3, that Statement nevertheless included a general recommendation that ". . . assets and lia-

---

[1] *Financial Reporting in Canada*—1973 edition—published by the CICA indicates that of the 325 companies included in the survey, 287 companies disclosed the existence of long-term debt which, in the case of 70 of those companies, was payable in foreign currency.

bilities that have both monetary and non-monetary characteristics should be classified as monetary or non-monetary based on the purpose for which they are held, usually evidenced by their treatment in historical-dollar accounting. . . ."

It is the authors' opinion that long-term debt payable in a foreign currency is an item that has monetary and non-monetary characteristics and therefore that this general recommendation should govern its classification. It is useful to consider this point in the light of the translation method used in the historical statements.

When long-term debt payable in a foreign currency has been translated in the historical cost statements at the current rate of exchange, the predominant characteristic is monetary. In the historical cost statements the long-term debt is regarded as similar to long-term debt in local currency, that is, as monetary. In the GPL statements the long-term debt should be classified as monetary; the same dollar amount will therefore appear in the historical cost and in the GPL statements.

When long-term debt payable in a foreign currency has been translated in the historical cost statements at the historical rate of exchange when the proceeds were received, the predominant characteristic is non-monetary. In the historical cost statements the long-term debt is regarded as a commodity; the liability for the debt is not adjusted to reflect changes in the exchange rate of the foreign currency. Long-term debt translated at the historical rate of exchange in the historical cost statements is treated in the same way as other non-monetary items; any gain or loss due to price changes is not recognized until an asset is sold or a liability is settled. Long-term debt payable in a foreign currency and carried in the historical cost statements at the historical rate of exchange is a non-monetary item for purposes of GPL accounting.

Accordingly, foreign currency long-term debt is restated each year by application of a conversion factor. When non-monetary assets are restated in GPL accounting, the resulting amount is compared with market value and recognition given to any impairment in value; the same principle applies to non-monetary liabilities. The amount of the long-term debt in foreign currency terms should be translated into the currency of the creditor (the local currency) at the current exchange rate; the restated amount in the GPL statements should not exceed this translated amount in local currency. (This is illustrated in the example on page 56.) The reduction of the GPL restated amount of the long-term debt to the local currency equivalent at the current rate of exchange is shown as a separate item in the GPL income statement.

Convertible debt

As an example of a liability having both monetary and non-monetary characteristics, APB Statement No. 3 cites convertible debt which ". . . is usually treated as straight debt and therefore is usually a monetary liability." However, if the conversion feature is predominant, the non-monetary characteristic should prevail and in the authors' opinion it is necessary to consider the features of each issue of convertible debt before classification is made. If there is a high degree of probability that the debt will be converted it should be classified as non-monetary; otherwise it should be treated as a monetary item.

Advances against sale or purchase contracts

In its exposure draft, the FASB has taken the position that advances paid on purchase contracts and advances received on sale contracts are non-monetary items, on the basis that the price of the goods to be received may fluctuate and consequently the advances are not claims to a fixed number of dollars. Some consideration of this point of view may be worthwhile. If the advances will be met by the delivery of goods of which the price is already known, the advances can be classified as non-monetary because in effect the amount relates to the goods although delivery has not yet been made. On the other hand, if the price of the goods may vary on or before delivery, it might be argued that the item in question is in fact the advance, and not the goods, and on that basis it would be more appropriate for the advance to be classified as a monetary item. This argument however does not recognize the substance of the transaction which is that a monetary item (the advance) has been exchanged for future delivery of a non-monetary item; therefore no further general price-level gain or loss can arise on the advance. There is however one proviso, namely that the contract may be avoidable and the advance refundable; if this is the case, and refund of the advance becomes probable, the advance should then be reclassified as a monetary item.

Non-monetary items carried at market value

Some non-monetary assets are commonly carried at market value in the historical cost financial statements; for example, investments held by mutual funds and other investment companies and some types of inventories, such as metal concentrates.

Non-monetary assets carried at market value in the historical financial statements would also be carried at market value in the GPL statements. In the case of investment companies the change in unrealized appreciation or depreciation during the year would be the difference between the market price at the beginning of the year, (restated into dollars of end-of-the-year purchasing power) and the market price at the end of the year, as already expressed in dollars of end-of-the-year purchasing power.

It could be said that non-monetary items carried at market value are already expressed in dollars of purchasing power at the end of the year and therefore do not require restatement, but this is an oversimplification of the actual application of GPL accounting. In fact, the non-monetary item is restated and the restated amount is then subjected to the realization test which requires the carrying amount to be reduced to market value by means of a charge against GPL income to provide for the diminution in value. It is considered preferable to disclose such GPL provision separately; if this is not done, the decrease in value is not identified and becomes an element of the general price-level gain or loss.

Limit to restatement of non-monetary assets

It was stated on page 2 that when the realization test is applied in historical cost statements, that same test must be applied in the GPL statements, and recognition given to any impairment in value. With items such as investments and inventories this does not create any special problems. The situation with regard to fixed assets is however different.

The write-down of fixed assets to recoverable or realizable value is an unsettled issue in historical cost accounting. In practice, if it is discovered at some point in the life of an asset that the depreciation practice adopted on acquisition of the asset is not adequate, it is changed for the remaining life of the asset. In some circumstances, the amount at which fixed assets are carried is reduced to recoverable value and a loss recorded prior to disposition of the assets. The circumstances in which such write-downs would be necessary are not explicitly defined in accounting literature but it is generally accepted that they do occur.

The question that arises and which is equally applicable to historical cost and GPL statements, is the assessment of the recoverable value to which the fixed assets should be reduced. Some companies, such as those in the public utility field, are concerned that the restated value of fixed assets on a GPL basis may exceed their recoverable value. Such companies are regulated as to the amounts they may charge their customers and the carrying value of their fixed assets has to be recovered through those rates charged to customers. One suggestion for a solution to this problem is that in organizations where revenue is governed by a regulatory body, any price-level gain on long-term debt should be excluded from GPL restated income and amortized over the life of the related fixed assets.

The authors believe it is unnecessary to adopt special accounting for such organizations because application of the normal principles of GPL accounting will achieve the necessary result. Most companies are faced with a ceiling on the amount they can charge for their product; it may be a rate imposed by a regulatory authority or simply the ceiling on the product price imposed by competition in the market place. Therefore in all companies the recoverable value of their fixed assets is linked to the proceeds from sale of their product to their customers.

In estimating the recoverable value of fixed assets to determine if the restated cost of fixed assets should be reduced to that recoverable value in the GPL statements it is necessary to look at the income flow, on a GPL basis, that will come from those assets. If the restated cost will be recoverable from the GPL adjusted income then no write-down would be necessary. The fact that the GPL restated cost of assets will not be recoverable from income calculated on the historical cost basis is not relevant.

The carrying value in the historical cost statements has to be recoverable from income calculated on the historical cost basis; the restated carrying value in the GPL statements has to be recoverable from income calculated on the GPL basis.

4

The Application of General Price-Level Accounting—Preparatory Steps

The decision to apply GPL accounting will have to be taken and certain preparatory work done before the year end selected for its introduction, if the GPL statements are to be available on a timely basis. The procedure for applying GPL accounting can best be illustrated by reference to a set of financial statements.

Assume that during 1974 the ABC Company decided that it would prepare GPL statements at December 31, 1974. The first step was to decide upon the general price index to be used and to obtain the indices for the relevant years and months. For the purposes of illustration, the following indices are used. These are assumed indices and have been expressed as whole numbers for the sake of convenience; as already explained, the conversion factors derived from them will be limited to three places of decimals.

Year	*Average index for year*	*Year*	*Average index for year*	*Index at December 31*
1940	48	1957	95	
1941	51	1958	96	
1942	53	1959	98	
1943	55	1960	99	
1944	56	1961	100	
1945	57	1962	101	
1946	59	1963	103	
1947	64	1964	104	
1948	72	1965	108	
1949	75	1966	112	
1950	78	1967	117	
1951	86	1968	122	
1952	88	1969	126	129
1953	89	1970	131	134
1954	90	1971	136	138
1955	91	1972	142	150
1956	93	1973	156	162

Monthly indices
1973

January	150	July	157
February	151	August	159
March	151	September	159
April	153	October	160
May	154	November	161
June	155	December	162

The preparation of GPL statements at December 31, 1974 for ABC Company will involve the following four stages:

1. Restatement of the 1973 historical cost balance sheet in dollars of December 1973 purchasing power. This step is necessary as a starting point for GPL accounting. It is essential to start from a base year and have all components of the balance sheet expressed in dollars of a uniform purchasing power.
2. Updating of the 1973 restated balance sheet (i.e. as prepared in 1) to dollars of December 1974 purchasing power.
3. Restatement of the 1974 historical cost balance sheet in dollars of December 1974 purchasing power.

4. Restatement of the 1974 historical cost income statement in dollars of December 1974 purchasing power.

In advance of December 31, 1974, the company began work on the restatement of its 1973 historical cost balance sheet into dollars of December 1973 purchasing power, and made such analyses as were necessary of its historical records, for example, fixed asset and accumulated depreciation accounts.

Exhibit A is the historical cost balance sheet of the company at December 31, 1973 that will be used in this example of GPL accounting. These statements are not consolidated financial statements; consolidated GPL statements will be dealt with in Chapters 7 to 9.

Restatement of 1973 historical balance sheet

The historical cost balance sheet at December 31, 1973 when restated so that all amounts are expressed in dollars of a uniform purchasing power will form the basis for all future GPL accounting. To prepare the 1973 GPL balance sheet, the first step is to identify the monetary items.

Identification and treatment of monetary items

Cash

Cash meets the criteria for a monetary item. In the historical financial statements the amount is already expressed in December 1973 dollars and the same amount is therefore entered in the GPL statements.

Exhibit A

ABC Company
Balance Sheet
December 31, 1973

	Historical cost basis
ASSETS	
Current assets:	
Cash	$ 1,660
Marketable securities	1,870
Accounts receivable	63,480
Inventories	98,560
Prepaid expenses	940
	$166,510
Investments:	
In associated companies	12,560
In unconsolidated subsidiary	10,000
Fixed assets:	
Buildings, machinery and equipment	340,910
Less: Accumulated depreciation	(113,290)
Land	6,560
Other assets:	
Unamortized issue expense of long-term debt	434
	$423,684
LIABILITIES AND SHAREHOLDERS' EQUITY	
Current liabilities:	
Bank loan	$ 10,230
Accounts payable	46,390
Income taxes	5,260
Current portion of long-term debt	370
	$ 62,250
Long-term debt	52,550
Deferred income taxes	43,250
Shareholders' equity:	
Share capital	80,450
Retained earnings	179,784
Excess of appraised value of assets over cost	5,400
	$423,684

Marketable securities

This account must be analyzed into its components to ascertain if any of the investments qualify as monetary items. Assume that this account consists of:

	Cost	*Market value*
Bonds and debentures		
7% debentures redeemable in 1980 at 100	$ 200	$ 200
7½ % debentures redeemable in 1984 at 98, 1985 at 99, 1986 at 100	300	300
Shares in listed companies	1,370	1,600
	$1,870	$2,100

As the bonds are redeemable at a fixed price they are classified as monetary; therefore the amount to be included in the price-level column is the same as in the historical cost column. The discount that would arise on early redemption is not recognized in the historical cost statements unless it occurs; the same treatment would be followed in the GPL statements. Similarly, a premium on redemption would be recognized in the GPL statements at the same time as in the historical statements. The marketable securities represented by shares in listed companies are classified as non-monetary items and will be dealt with on page 39.

Accounts receivable

These represent items where the dollar amount is fixed and so meet the criteria for monetary items. Any allowance for doubtful accounts deducted from the receivables does not alter the nature of the item. The amount of accounts receivable less any allowance for doubtful accounts is shown in the same amount for GPL purposes as in the historical statements.

Bank loan, accounts payable, and income taxes

These items are fixed as to the dollar amount payable and so meet the criteria for monetary items.

Long-term debt

Assume that this account consists of:

Sinking fund debentures, class "A" due 1995		$22,250
Sinking fund debentures, class "B" due 1995 in a foreign currency (FC $28,400)		30,670
		$52,920
Less portion included in current liabilities		
"A" debentures	$171	
"B" debentures	199	370
		$52,550

The class "A" debentures are not payable in a different currency and therefore are classified as a monetary item. $171 is included in current liabilities and the balance of $22,079 is entered in the price-level column for long-term debt. As discussed earlier, the debentures payable in a foreign currency have characteristics of both monetary and non-monetary items, but, when translated at the historical rate of exchange, are considered to be non-monetary. These are accordingly restated each year and the restated amount is then compared with the local currency equivalent at the current rate of exchange of the amount repayable in the foreign currency. The liability is not restated above the amount repayable when translated at the current rate of exchange. (See page 56.)

Deferred income taxes

For the reasons discussed on pages 18 *et seq* this item is classified as monetary.

Share capital

Assume the issued share capital of the company is represented by:

10,000 5% preferred shares, redeemable in 1980, at 102	$10,000
10,000 5% preferred shares, convertible to common shares 1978 to 1980	10,000
60,450 common shares of no par value	60,450
	$80,450

The preferred shares redeemable in 1980 are classified as monetary, on the basis of their being redeemable, although as explained on page 17 the classification is of relatively little practical importance in this example because the price-level gain on the shares will be carried to shareholders' equity.

In this example it is assumed the convertible preferred shares will be converted into common shares during the conversion period, so they are classified as non-monetary. The remainder of the issued share capital, the common shares, is non-monetary and is discussed and dealt with on page 57.

When all the monetary items have been identified, the amounts will appear in the working price-level balance sheet shown in Exhibit B.

Identification and treatment of non-monetary items

The non-monetary items must now be restated in terms of purchasing power at the balance sheet date. These items are analyzed to show costs and dates of acquisition in order that they can be restated on a price-level basis by use of appropriate conversion factors.

Exhibit B

ABC Company
Balance Sheet
December 31, 1973

	Historical	*Price-level*
ASSETS		
Current assets:		
Cash	$ 1,660	$ 1,660
Marketable securities	1,870	500
Accounts receivable	63,480	63,480
Inventories	98,560	
Prepaid expenses	940	
	$166,510	
Investments:		
In associated companies	12,560	
In unconsolidated subsidiary	10,000	
Fixed assets:		
Buildings, machinery and equipment	340,910	
Less: Accumulated depreciation	(113,290)	
Land	6,560	
Other assets:		
Unamortized issue expense of long-term debt	434	
	$423,684	
LIABILITIES AND SHAREHOLDERS' EQUITY		
Current liabilities:		
Bank loan	$ 10,230	$10,230
Accounts payable	46,390	46,390
Income taxes	5,260	5,260
Current portion of long-term debt	370	370
	$ 62,250	$62,250
Long-term debt	52,550	22,079
Deferred income taxes	43,250	43,250
Shareholders' equity:		
Share capital	80,450	10,000
Retained earnings	179,784	
Excess of appraised value of assets over cost	5,400	
	$423,684	

Marketable securities

	Cost	*Market value*
Shares in listed companies:		
X Company – acquired by several purchases in 1966	$ 568	$ 700
Y Company – acquired by several purchases in 1968	646	725
Z Company – acquired in June 1970	156	175
	$1,370	$1,600

These investments are not accounted for by the equity method. The conversion factors applicable to these investments are·

$$1966 \quad \frac{\text{December 1973 index}}{\text{Average 1966 index}} = \frac{162}{112} = 1.446$$

$$1968 \quad \frac{\text{December 1973 index}}{\text{Average 1968 index}} = \frac{162}{122} = 1.328$$

$$1970 \quad \frac{\text{December 1973 index}}{\text{Average 1970 index}} = \frac{162}{131} = 1.237$$

The average indices for 1966 and 1968 are used because the shares were acquired as the result of several purchases in the two years. In the case of the investment in Z Company, it is acceptable to use the average index of the year, as explained on page 5.

The marketable securities account can now be restated.

	Historical	*Conversion factor*	*Price-level 1973 $*	*Market value*
X Company	$ 568	1.446	$ 821	$ 700
Y Company	646	1.328	858	725
Z Company	156	1.237	193	175
	$1,370		$1,872	$1,600

It has already been noted that the GPL statements are based on the same accounting principles as the historical statements. In this case the carrying value in the GPL statements, but not in the historical cost statements, is in excess of market value. As these are temporary investments, the carrying value in the GPL balance sheet is restricted to the market value, i.e. $1,600.

Inventories

Restatement of inventories to reflect price-level change depends on the bases on which such inventories are recorded in the historical cost financial statements. Whether the cost of inventory is calculated at invoice cost or by an average, weighted average, FIFO, LIFO, or base stock method, the conversion factors to apply will be those corresponding to the dates on which such costs were incurred.

The restatement of non-monetary items must not result in their being shown in price-level statements at amounts in excess of their recoverable value. Accordingly, the basic rule of lower of cost and market must be applied. Inventories should not be stated at more than their market value, market value being interpreted for each class of inventory in exactly the same way as it is interpreted in the historical cost statements.

If inventories have been stated in the historical cost statement at net realizable value which is lower than historical cost, the same procedure applies as described on page 28: it is necessary first to restate the inventories, and then to make a provision by means of a charge against GPL income to reduce the inventories to their net realizable value. In other words, although inventories will thus be stated in the GPL balance sheet in the same amount as in the historical balance sheet, it remains necessary to follow the restatement and provision approach so as to identify the effect in GPL income.

If an asset, such as inventory, is reduced below the GPL restated cost so that the carrying value is restricted to "market" or recoverable value, the reduction, in the base year of GPL accounting, is achieved by adjusting the retained earnings resulting from the initial restatement. In subsequent years the reduction to market value is charged in the GPL income statement.

The analysis of the inventories in the December 1973 historical balance sheet of ABC Company is:

Raw materials	$30,245
Work in process	18,077
Finished goods	50,238
	$98,560

Raw materials are carried at cost determined on a first-in first-out basis, and are assumed to represent costs accumulated more or less evenly over the last four months of the year; therefore an average conversion factor, based on the last five month-end indices in the year, can be applied. Work in process is carried at average cost with costs accumulated over the last six months of the year. Finished goods are carried at average cost with costs accumulated over the last six months of the year. On these assumptions, conversion factors for each category of inventory would be calculated as follows:

Raw materials

$$\frac{\text{December 1973 month-end index}}{\text{Average of August to December 1973 month-end indices}}$$

$$= \frac{162}{(159 + 159 + 160 + 161 + 162) \div 5}$$

$$= \frac{162}{160.2} = 1.011$$

Work in process

$$\frac{\text{December 1973 month-end index}}{\text{Average of June to December 1973 month-end indices}}$$

$$= \frac{162}{(155 + 157 + 159 + 159 + 160 + 161 + 162) \div 7}$$

$$= \frac{162}{159} = 1.019$$

Finished goods

These are assumed to have accumulated over the same period as work in process, that is, the last six months of the year, and the same conversion factor is therefore used.

The inventories account can now be restated.

	Historical	*Conversion factor*	*Price-level 1973 $*	*Net realizable value*
Raw materials	$30,245	1.011	$ 30,578	$ 36,150
Work in process	18,077	1.019	18,420	22,100
Finished goods	50,238	1.019	51,193	55,400
	$98,560		$100,191	$113,650

It has been assumed that depreciation included in the cost of overhead expenses allocated to inventories is not sufficiently material to warrant separate analysis. If depreciation were material, the same conversion factors as are used for its restatement elsewhere in the accounts would be used, and the balance of the inventory amounts would be converted in the same manner as shown above.

If raw materials had been carried on the last-in first-out (LIFO) method, the GPL restatement would have been approached in a different manner. It would be necessary, first, to analyze the raw materials account on the historical basis to determine the years of acquisition of each "layer" of inventory remaining on hand at December 31, 1973. The appropriate conversion factors would then be applied to each layer to arrive at the restated total at December 31, 1973.

Prepaid expenses

The analysis of prepaid expenses in the 1973 historical statements is as follows:

Unexpired insurance	$320
Prepaid advertising	470
Prepaid interest (not paid before due date)	150
	$940

Prepaid expenses are non-monetary. If, however, interest is paid before it is due and an accounting date occurs between the date of payment and the due date, it is classified as a monetary item at the accounting date.

Prepaid expenses were incurred in the following months:

1973	*Unamortized balance at December 31, 1973*	*Conversion factor*	*Price-level 1973 $*
May	$270	162/154, or 1.052	$284
October	420	162/160, or 1.013	425
December	250	162/162, or 1.000	250
	$940		$959

Investments in associated companies

The investment account is represented by:

		Market value
Investment in DEF Ltd., at cost	$ 1,100	$ 1,400
Investment in GHI Ltd., at equity	9,960	14,000
Advance to GHI Ltd.	1,500	—
	$12,560	

The allocation of intercompany accounts, such as advances, into monetary and non-monetary groups should be based on the time repayment is expected and not necessarily on their classification in the separate financial statements of each corporation. Advances from an investor to an investee should be regarded as non-monetary if there is no expectation that the advances will be repaid; they represent additional long-term investments by the investor.

Investments in other companies carried on the cost basis, i.e. portfolio investments, are classified as non-monetary. Investments in joint ventures accounted for on a proportionate line-by-line basis do not create any particular problems in classification or restatement; the share of the assets, liabilities, revenue and expenses of the joint venture will be merged with similar items in the joint venturer's financial statements and updated as part of those items.

When investments in other companies and in joint ventures are carried on the equity basis, they cannot be restated on a GPL basis simply by applying conversion factors to the cost and to each year's share of earnings. In order to apply GPL accounting to investments and joint ventures carried on the equity basis it is necessary to obtain GPL statements of the investee at the date of acquisition of the investment and for each subsequent accounting period.

The statements at the date of acquisition of the investment are necessary so that the cost of the investment can be compared with the GPL restated amount of the net assets acquired and the goodwill figure calculated. If the cost of the investment were compared with the net assets acquired based on the historical cost of the investee's balance sheet, one would be comparing cost, in dollars of value at acquisition date, with net assets, in dollars of value at varying dates.

GPL statements of the investee for years subsequent to the date of acquisition are required in order that the investor's share of income, based on the GPL statements of the investee, is included in the investor's GPL income statement.

It is emphasized that GPL restated accounts of the investee are necessary when the investor accounts on the equity basis. The fact that either the investment or the income from the investee in the historical cost statements may not be material does not remove this necessity. The investment and share of income may differ materially on restatement from their amounts in the historical cost statements; historical retained earnings could even become a deficit in GPL statements. The situation when GPL statements are unavailable is discussed on page 102.

In applying GPL accounting to the investment account of ABC Company the individual investments have to be considered.

The investment in DEF Ltd. is carried on the cost basis. It was acquired in 1965 and its cost can be restated as follows:

	Historical	*Conversion factor*	*Price-level 1973 $*	*Market value*
Investment in DEF Ltd.	$1,100	162/108, or 1.500	$1,650	$1,400

This is another situation in which the amount on a GPL adjusted basis exceeds market value, although market value is still in excess of historical cost. However, unlike the marketable securities already discussed, these are long-term investments and the question therefore arises as to whether or not there is considered to be a permanent impairment of the value of the investment. In this example it is assumed that no permanent impairment of value has occurred at this time. (See page 71 for treatment in 1974 when impairment is assumed to have occurred.) The investment in DEF Ltd. is therefore carried in the 1973 GPL balance sheet at its restated cost of $1,650 in 1973 dollars.

In considering the investment in GHI Ltd., it is assumed the advance has been made on a long-term basis; because there is no expectation that it will be repaid, it is treated as a non-monetary item.

Date advanced	*Historical*	*Conversion factor*	*Price-level 1973 $*
1969	$1,000	162/126, or 1.286	$1,286
1970	500	162/131, or 1.237	618
	$1,500		$1,904

The average indices for 1969 and 1970 have been used as a matter of convenience.

The investment in GHI Ltd. was acquired in December 1969 so it is necessary to reconstruct the investment account on both a historical cost and GPL basis from that date forward.

In December 1969, a 40% interest in GHI Ltd. showed:

		40%
Net assets on historical cost basis	$17,750	$7,100
Net assets on GPL basis in 1969 dollars	$20,460	$8,184

A 40% interest in the net assets would therefore amount to $7,100 on the historical cost basis and to $8,184 in 1969 dollars on the GPL basis.

At the date of acquisition, the investing company's purchase price is compared with its 40% share of the net assets of GHI Ltd. and the goodwill included in the purchase price can be calculated on the historical and GPL bases.

	Historical	*Price-level 1969 $*
Purchase price	$8,450	$8,450
Net assets	7,100	8,184
	$1,350	$ 266

The changes in the investment accounts from the date of acquisition to December 1973 are then analyzed on both the historical and GPL bases.

	Historical		*Price-level*	
	Goodwill	*Net assets*	*Goodwill*	*Net assets*
December 1969 opening balance	$1,350	$7,100	$266	$ 8,184
December 1970				
Restated to December 1970 dollars 134/129, or 1.039			$276	$ 8,503
40% interest in earnings of GHI Ltd. for 1971 on historical basis		258		
*on price-level basis				124
	$1,350	$7,358	$276	$ 8,627

*These figures are obtained from the price-level adjusted income statement of GHI Ltd. for each year.

	Historical		*Price-level*	
	Goodwill	*Net assets*	*Goodwill*	*Net assets*
December 1971				
Restated to December 1971 dollars 138/134, or 1.030			$284	$ 8,886
40% interest in earnings of GHI Ltd. for 1971				
on historical basis		368		
*on price-level basis				195
	$1,350	$7,726	$284	$ 9,081
December 1972				
Restated to December 1972 dollars 150/138, or 1.087			$309	$ 9,871
40% interest in earnings of GHI Ltd. for 1972				
on historical basis		460		
*on price-level basis				245
	$1,350	$8,186	$309	$10,116
December 1973				
Restated to December 1973 dollars 162/150, or 1.080			$334	$10,925
40% interest in earnings of GHI Ltd. for 1973				
on historical basis		424		
*on price-level basis				225
	$1,350	8,610	$334	11,150
		1,350		334
		$9,960		$11,484

*These figures are obtained from the price-level adjusted income statement of GHI Ltd. for each year.

When the restated cost of the investment in GHI Ltd. has been established at $11,484 in 1973 dollars it must be compared with market or recoverable value at that date to ascertain if any provision for diminution in value is required. The market value at December 1973 is $14,000 and no provision for impairment is necessary.

Goodwill has not been amortized and so remains unchanged in the historical cost statement. In the GPL statements the goodwill is a non-monetary item and must be restated each year, but it is not amortized unless the policy with regard to goodwill in the historical cost statements is changed.

Before leaving the subject of these investments, consider what the effect would have been if GPL statements of GHI Ltd. had not been obtained but the conversion factors had merely been applied to historical figures.

Investment in GHI Ltd. December 1969 at cost	$ 8,450
Updated to December 1973	
$8,450 × 162/129, or 1.256	$10,613
Share of earnings each year	
1970 $258 × 162/131, or 1.237	319
1971 $368 × 162/136, or 1.191	438
1972 $460 × 162/142, or 1.141	525
1973 $424 × 162/156, or 1.038	440
	$12,335

If this "simple" basis had been used, the investment account would have been overstated by $851 ($12,335 less $11,484).

Investment in unconsolidated subsidiary

In the corporate statements, the investment in the subsidiary is carried on the cost basis. A discussion of the application of GPL accounting to consolidated financial statements is contained in Chapters 7 to 9. The investment in LMN Company Ltd., as it is carried on the cost basis, is classified as a non-monetary item and updated from the date of acquisition. Because the subsidiary's accounts have been restated each year for GPL purposes, this updating has to be made year by year, rather than in the ratio of 1971 to 1973 indices, to permit consolidation.

	Historical	*Conversion factors 1972 and 1973*	*Price-level 1972 and 1973 $*	*Market value*
Investment in LMN Company Ltd. acquired in 1971	$10,000	150/138, or 1.087	$10,870	$15,000
		162/150, or 1.080	11,740	15,000

Fixed assets

The costs and accumulated depreciation relating to fixed assets should be analyzed according to years of purchase for each main depreciation category. It will not be necessary to analyze these accounts for each class of fixed assets beyond the dates of acquisition of assets which have not yet been fully depreciated. If there are fully depreciated assets still in use, it will generally be sufficient to group these and apply a conversion factor appropriate to an average date of acquisition. The cost of assets disposed of should be deducted from the expenditure of the years in which they were acquired, so that there remains an aged analysis of fixed assets held and the related accumulated depreciation. Where this information cannot be obtained from a plant ledger, a regressive analysis of expenditures should be made to the extent practical so as to obtain an acceptable estimate.

Restatement of appraised values

In some cases a company may consider basing its GPL adjustments of fixed assets upon an appraisal which has been made, for example, for insurance purposes but which has not been recorded in the accounts. There is a basic objection to the use of an appraisal as a starting point for GPL adjustments of fixed assets in place of historical cost amounts because it would introduce a different application of an accounting principle in the GPL statements to that used in the historical statements. Reference has already been made to the fact that GPL accounting must adhere to the same principles as historical cost accounting; it is not sufficient to adhere to acceptable alternative accounting principles. If an appraised value is used in the historical statements, it must also be used as the basis for GPL accounting; if cost is used in the historical statements, it must also be used for GPL accounting.

When an appraisal of fixed assets has been recorded in the historical accounts in a year prior to the adoption of GPL accounting, the appraised value will have been substituted for the historical cost of the assets, less depreciation accumulated to the date of appraisal. This appraised amount takes the place of the historical cost of the asset, and the conversion factor appropriate to the date of the appraisal is used to restate the cost of the asset for GPL statements.

The excess of appraised value over cost arising from the appraisal is calculated in the historical statements by reference to the appraised amount and the depreciated cost. In the GPL statements the appraisal credit is calculated by reference to the appraisal amount and the original cost less accumulated depreciation, restated to dollars of purchasing power value at the date of the appraisal. This achieves a comparison of the appraised amount, in dollars of value at the appraisal date, with restated cost, in dollars of value at the same date.

When an appraisal of fixed assets is recorded in the historical accounts after the adoption of GPL accounting, the appraised amount takes the place of the historical cost of the asset. If the appraisal is made at the year end, the appraised value is substituted in the GPL statements for the restated net cost of the asset, that is, restated cost less restated depreciation accumulated to the date of the appraisal. When the appraisal takes place during a financial year, the restated cost less restated depreciation and the appraised amount are updated into dollars of purchasing power as at the end of the financial year. The appraisal increase credit is calculated for GPL purposes by comparing the appraised amount, expressed in dollars of value at the end of the financial year, with the restated cost less accumulated depreciation also expressed in dollars of value at the end of the financial year.

The effect in the GPL statements of calculating an appraisal credit by reference to the original cost of the asset, as restated to the date of the appraisal, is reflected only in the amount of retained earnings. The appraisal increase credit remains indefinitely as part of shareholders' equity or may be transferred to retained earnings in amounts not exceeding the realization of the appraisal through sale or depreciation provisions. The amount attributed to the appraisal credit does not flow through to the income statement.

The amount attributed to the appraisal increase credit therefore affects only the amount shown as the balance of retained earnings which will be explained later on page 58 is a residual figure in the price-level balance sheet for the base year preparatory to the adoption of GPL accounting. Similarly, in each future year the restatement of the appraisal increase credit will have no effect other than on the balance of retained earnings on the GPL basis. The restatement of the appraisal increase credit therefore affects two elements of shareholders' equity by offsetting amounts and for this reason there may appear to be little practical advantage in restating the appraisal credit. The point has been mentioned here, however, to show the nature and effect of GPL accounting in this instance. It may also be noted that when the appraised amount is compared with the restated cost, an appraisal credit in the historical statements may be converted into an appraisal "debit" in the GPL statements. In such circumstances the appraisal increase debit in the GPL statements would be offset against the amount of retained earnings.

Capitalization of carrying charges

When interest and other carrying charges are capitalized as part of the historical cost of fixed assets, the same procedure is followed in GPL accounting. In most cases the amount of interest capitalized will be less than the total interest expense. The restated interest expense (calculated by applying the average or weighted average conversion factor for the year—see page 92) is prorated and the proportion equivalent to the amount capitalized in historical cost is added to the asset cost for price-level purposes. No part of the price-level gain arising from the related debt is offset against the restated asset because such gain relates to the existence of debt irrespective of the use made of the proceeds of the debt.

When the total interest expense or any other carrying charge is capitalized as part of the historical cost of assets, no proration is necessary. The total expense as restated for GPL purposes is included in the restated cost of the assets.

Property, plant and equipment

The breakdown of the property, plant and equipment account of ABC Company at December 31, 1973 was:

	Cost	*Accumulated depreciation*
Land, at appraised value	$ 6,560	–
Buildings, at appraised value in 1965 and subsequent additions at cost	$ 20,450	$ 4,389
Machinery and equipment, at cost	310,870	104,236
Furniture and fixtures, at cost	9,590	4,665
	$340,910	$113,290

For GPL purposes it is generally preferable to restate acquisitions of fixed assets in the current year by reference to the actual monthly or quarterly index; or, when dealing with acquisitions made in prior years it is generally adequate to use the average index of the year concerned. In following this approach in the present instance, average annual indices will be used to restate property, plant and equipment on hand at December 31, 1973.

For the purposes of illustration, the following assumptions are made:

Depreciation on straight-line basis.*
Full years depreciation in year of acquisition.

---

*The calculation of the annual provision on a price-level basis is explained in connection with restating the current year's fixed asset and accumulated depreciation accounts on pages 74 *et seq.* The restatement of annual provisions when depreciation in the historical statements is calculated by other than the straight-line method is dealt with on page 92.

No depreciation in year of disposal.
Useful lives: 40 years for buildings.
20 years for machinery and equipment.
10 years for furniture and fixtures.
No salvage value.

Land

The land is carried at the 1965 appraised value. The original date of acquisition and original cost are no longer relevant to the asset account although they are still relevant to the calculation, on both historical and GPL bases, of the appraisal increase credit.

To restate the asset account for GPL purposes, the appraised value in 1965 is taken as if it were the "cost" of the land and is updated by the conversion factor applicable to 1965 additions.

	Cost	*Conversion factor*	*Price-level 1973 $*
Land, at appraised value	$6,560	162/108, or 1.500	$9,840

Depreciable fixed assets

When the asset accounts have been analyzed (or estimated) by years of acquisition, the accumulated depreciation can be calculated as the appropriate percentage of cost. Conversion factors using the average indices for each year are then applied. This is shown in Figure 4.1.

The GPL adjusted figures can now be summarized and entered in the price-level column of the balance sheet.

	Price-level 1973 $	
	Cost	*Accumulated depreciation*
Buildings	$ 30,198	$ 6,503
Machinery and equipment	422,256	152,510
Furniture and fixtures	12,238	6,324
	$464,692	$165,337

Figure 4.1

	Historical balances at December 31, 1973				Price-level 1973 $	
Buildings	*Cost*	*Percentage depreciated*	*Accumulated depreciation*	*Conversion factor*	*Cost*	*Depreciation*
1965, appraised value	$ 15,450	22.5%	$ 3,476	162/108, or 1.500	$ 23,175	$ 5,214
1966	3,250	20.0	650	162/112 1.446	4,699	940
1968	1,750	15.0	263	162/122 1.328	2,324	349
	$ 20,450		$ 4,389		$ 30,198	$ 6,503
Machinery and equipment						
1954	$ 1,570	100%	$ 1,570	162/90, or 1.800	$ 2,826	$ 2,826
1956	6,428	90	5,785	162/93 1.742	11,198	10,077
1958	7,468	80	5,974	162/96 1.688	12,606	10,084
1960	8,480	70	5,936	162/99 1.636	13,873	9,711
1962	9,568	60	5,741	162/101 1.604	15,347	9,209
1963	14,432	55	7,938	162/103 1.573	22,702	12,486
1964	15,469	50	7,734	162/104 1.558	24,101	12,050
1965	26,248	45	11,812	162/108 1.500	39,372	17,718
1966	27,165	40	10,866	162/112 1.446	39,281	15,712
1967	28,432	35	9,951	162/117 1.385	39,378	13,782
1968	30,600	30	9,180	162/122 1.328	40,637	12,191
1969	31,250	25	7,813	162/126 1.286	40,187	10,047
1970	32,145	20	6,429	162/131 1.237	39,763	7,953
1971	27,168	15	4,075	162/136 1.191	32,357	4,853
1972	24,200	10	2,420	162/142 1.141	27,612	2,761
1973	20,247	5	1,012	162/156 1.038	21,016	1,050
	$310,870		$104,236		$422,256	$152,510

Figure 4.1 (continued)

	Historical balances at December 31, 1973				Price-level 1973 $	
Furniture and fixtures	*Cost*	*Percentage depreciated*	*Accumulated depreciation*	*Conversion factor*	*Cost*	*Depreciation*
1964	$ 340	100%	$ 340	162/104, or 1.558	$ 530	$ 530
1965	740	90	666	162/108 1.500	1,110	999
1966	850	80	680	162/112 1.446	1,229	983
1967	1,029	70	720	162/117 1.385	1,425	997
1968	1,080	60	648	162/122 1.328	1,434	861
1969	960	50	480	162/126 1.286	1,235	617
1970	1,045	40	418	162/131 1.237	1,293	517
1971	1,268	30	381	162/136 1.191	1,510	454
1972	1,042	20	208	162/142 1.141	1,189	237
1973	1,236	10	124	162/156 1.038	1,283	129
	$ 9,590		$ 4,665		$ 12,238	$ 6,324

Unamortized issue expense on long-term debt

The unamortized issue expense on long-term debt relates to the debentures outstanding and is being amortized over their 30 year life. Although the liability for the outstanding debt is classified as a monetary item, the issue expense, as with most deferred charges, represents a cost incurred in the past which will be charged against future income and is therefore non-monetary.

	Historical	*Conversion factor*	*Price-level 1973 $*
Issue expense in 1965	$620	162/108, or 1.500	$930
Amortized to 1973	186		279
	$434		$651

It may be noted that if long-term debt has been issued at a discount, the discount has the same characteristics as the debt itself and is considered a monetary item.

Long-term debt

The debentures payable in a foreign currency are classified as non-monetary (page 36) and must be restated. The debt was incurred in 1965, when FC $30,000 was borrowed. The sinking fund provisions of FC $200 per year from 1966 to 1973 have reduced the amount outstanding at December 1973 to FC $28,400. The amount borrowed in 1965 expressed in local currency was $32,342 reduced by sinking fund provisions to the amount outstanding at December 1973 of $30,670.

	Historical			*Price-level*	*Translated*
	FC $	*Local $*	*Conversion factor*	*1973 Local $*	*at current rate*
Incurred 1965	FC $30,000	$32,342			
Sinking Fund	1,600	1,672			
Balance 1973	FC $28,400	$30,670	162/108, or 1.500	$46,005	$28,281

The amount to which the debt can be restated in the GPL accounts is restricted to the equivalent of the amount repayable in foreign currency translated at the current rate of exchange which at December 1973 has been assumed to be FC $1.00 = Local currency $0.9958. The liability in the GPL statement is therefore restricted to the local currency amount of $28,281. The portion included in current liabilities has already been translated at the current rate so the restated amounts of long-term debt are $28,281 less $199 or $28,082.

Share capital

The monetary items in issued share capital have already been discussed on page 37 and the other two classes of share capital remain to be considered.

10,000 5% preferred shares convertible to common shares 1978 to 1980	$10,000
60,450 common shares, no par value	$60,450

	Historical	*Conversion factor*	*Price-level 1973 $*
Preferred shares			
Issued 1963	$10,000	162/103, or 1.573	$ 15,730
Common shares			
Issued 1940	$10,500	162/48, or 3.375	$ 35,437
1950	20,500	162/78, or 2.077	42,579
1955	15,000	162/91, or 1.780	26,700
1960	14,450	162/99, or 1.636	23,640
	$60,450		$128,356

Some accountants do not consider it necessary to distinguish between common share capital and retained earnings in GPL accounting. Other accountants feel that it is desirable to preserve the distinction. As the two accounts are not merged in the historical cost statements, there is perhaps some advantage in preserving that distinction in the GPL adjusted statements; the point is essentially one of presentation.

Excess of appraised value over cost

The excess of appraised value over cost is the credit arising from the appraisal of land and buildings in 1965. To restate this excess it is necessary to obtain the original cost and accumulated depreciation of the appraised assets and update those amounts into dollars of purchasing power value at the date of the appraisal. The restated cost less accumulated depreciation, expressed in 1965 dollars, is then compared with the appraised amount, expressed in 1965 dollars, to obtain the amount of the appraisal credit arising in 1965 expressed in GPL terms.

	Cost less accumulated depreciation	*Original acquisition date*	*Conversion factor*	*Price-level 1965 $*	*Appraised value 1965 $*	*Appraisal credit 1965 $*
Land	$ 3,000	1950	162/78, or 2.077	$ 6,231	$ 6,560	$ 329
Building	13,610	1950	162/78, or 2.077	28,268	15,450	(12,818)
	$16,610			$34,499	$22,010	$(12,489)

	Appraisal credit 1965 $	*Conversion factor*	*Price-level 1973 $*
Appraisal credit, arising 1965	($12,489)	162/108, or 1.500	$(18,734)

It will be noted that the effect of the restatement is to change the appraisal credit into a debit balance for GPL purposes. This appraisal increase "debit" is not shown separately in the GPL statements, but is set off against the amount attributed to retained earnings.

Retained earnings

The balance of retained earnings is considered as a residual for purposes of GPL accounting and is not classified as a monetary or non-monetary item. The balance shown as retained earnings in the first balance sheet adjusted to a GPL basis is the balancing figure between the aggregate of the liabilities and share capital on one hand and total assets on the other, after all items have been restated to dollars of the same purchasing power. The effect of restating the assets and other items into dollars of the same purchasing power results in an adjustment of retained earnings.

When GPL accounting is first adopted, the income statement for the base year is not restated; it follows that in the GPL adjusted balance sheet of the base year the retained earnings can be expressed only as a residual figure. In Chapter 6 it will be seen that in the following and subsequent years the balance of retained earnings in the GPL adjusted statements flows through from the GPL adjusted income statements.

Exhibit C

ABC Company
Balance Sheet
December 31, 1973

	Historical	*Price-level*	*Page reference*
ASSETS			
Current assets:			
Cash	$ 1,660	$ 1,660	33
Marketable securities	1,870	500	35
		1,600	39
Accounts receivable	63,480	63,480	35
Inventories	98,560	100,191	42
Prepaid expenses	940	959	42
	$166,510	$168,390	
Investments:			
In associated companies	12,560	1,650	45
		1,904	45
		11,484	46
In unconsolidated subsidiary	10,000	11,740	49
Fixed assets:			
Buildings, machinery and equipment	340,910	464,692	53
Less: Accumulated depreciation	(113,290)	(165,337)	53
Land	6,560	9,840	53
Other assets:			
Unamortized issue expense of long-term debt	434	651	56
	$423,684	$505,014	

Exhibit C (continued)

	Historical	*Price-level*	*Page reference*
LIABILITIES AND SHAREHOLDERS' EQUITY			
Current liabilities:			
Bank loan	$ 10,230	$ 10,230	35
Accounts payable	46,390	46,390	35
Income taxes	5,260	5,260	35
Current portion of long-term debt	370	370	36
	$ 62,250	$ 62,250	
Long-term debt	52,550	22,079	36
		28,082	57
Deferred income taxes	43,250	43,250	36
Shareholders' equity:			
Share capital	80,450	10,000	37
		15,730	57
		128,356	57
Retained earnings	179,784	195,267	58
Excess of appraised value of assets over cost	5,400	—	58
	$423,684	$505,014	

5

Restating the Current Balance Sheet

The next stages in the preparation of GPL statements at December 31, 1974 by ABC Company are as follows:

- Updating the 1973 restated balance sheet to dollars of December 31, 1974 purchasing power
- Restating the 1974 historical balance sheet to dollars of December 31, 1974 purchasing power.

Obviously none of these steps can be taken until the 1974 price-level indices are known and the 1974 historical statements have been prepared.

The following are the assumed 1974 price-level indices that will be used in the example.

Monthly indices, 1974

January	163	July	175
February	165	August	177
March	167	September	179
April	169	October	181
May	171	November	183
June	173	December	185

Annual average 174

Updating the 1973 restated balance sheet

To make GPL statements prepared at different dates comparable, the GPL statement for the comparative year must be updated. In the case of ABC Company the restated balance sheet of the base year 1973 will have served its purpose when it has been updated, but it cannot be used as the starting point for the 1974 GPL statements until it has been translated into dollars of December 31, 1974 purchasing power.

This updating is done very simply by rolling forward all the dollar figures in the 1973 restated balance sheet. Each amount is multiplied by the conversion factor, being the index number at the end of the current accounting period divided by the index number at the end of the previously reported accounting period. In this case the index number at December 31, 1974 was 185 and at December 31, 1973 was 162. The conversion factor is 185/162, or 1.142.

Cash, for example, when expressed in 1973 dollars amounts to $1,660 and application of the conversion factor restates this amount at $1,896 in terms of 1974 dollars. Similarly, inventories are restated at $100,191 × 1.142 = $114,418. Note that the updating is applied to all items, regardless of whether they are monetary or non-monetary.

The GPL balance sheet at December 31, 1973 is shown as Exhibit D together with the equivalent amounts when it is rolled forward to December 31, 1974 dollars.

Restating the 1974 historical balance sheet

The unconsolidated balance sheet of ABC Company at December 31, 1974 prepared on a historical cost basis is shown as Exhibit E.

The first stage in restating the 1974 balance sheet is basically similar to the restatement of the 1973 balance sheet. The monetary items are segregated and entered into the price-level column. The

Exhibit D

ABC Company
GPL Balance Sheet
December 31, 1973

	Expressed in 1973 $	*Expressed in 1974 $*
ASSETS		
Current assets:		
Cash	$ 1,660	$ 1,896
Marketable securities	2,100	2,398
Accounts receivable	63,480	72,494
Inventories	100,191	114,418
Prepaid expenses	959	1,095
	$168,390	$192,301
Investments:		
In associated companies	15,038	17,173
In unconsolidated subsidiary	11,740	13,407
Fixed assets:		
Buildings, machinery and equipment	464,692	530,678
Less: Accumulated depreciation	(165,337)	(188,815)
Land	9,840	11,237
Other assets:		
Unamortized issue expenses of long-term debt	651	744
	$505,014	$576,725

	Expressed in 1973 $	*Expressed in 1974 $*
LIABILITIES AND SHAREHOLDERS' EQUITY		
Current liabilities:		
Bank loan	$ 10,230	$ 11,683
Accounts payable	46,390	52,977
Income taxes	5,260	6,007
Current portion of long-term debt	370	422
	$ 62,250	$ 71,089
Long-term debt	50,161	57,284
Deferred income taxes	43,250	49,391
Shareholders' equity:		
Share capital	154,086	175,966
Retained earnings	195,267	222,995
	$505,014	$576,725

Exhibit E

ABC Company
Balance Sheet
December 31, 1974

	Historical Cost Basis
ASSETS	
Current assets:	
Cash	$ 5,590
Marketable securities	2,250
Accounts receivable	61,580
Inventories	96,050
Prepaid expenses	870
	$166,340
Investments:	
In associated companies	13,110
In unconsolidated subsidiary	10,000
Fixed assets:	
Buildings, machinery and equipment	362,110
Less: Accumulated depreciation	(122,184)
Land	6,560
Other assets:	
Unamortized issue expense of long-term debt	413
	$436,349
LIABILITIES AND SHAREHOLDERS' EQUITY	
Current liabilities:	
Bank loan	$ 5,160
Accounts payable	49,680
Income taxes	5,760
Current portion of long-term debt	370
	$ 60,970
Long-term debt	52,180
Deferred income taxes	49,680
Shareholders' equity:	
Share capital	80,450
Retained earnings	187,669
Excess of appraised value of assets over cost	5,400
	$436,349

monetary items are again cash, accounts receivable, bank loan, accounts payable, income taxes, current portion of the long-term debt, long-term debt payable in local currency and deferred income taxes. The question of the marketable securities and the preferred shares which were monetary items in the December 1973 balance sheet cannot be determined until the analysis is made of the marketable securities account and the share capital account in the December 1974 historical cost balance sheet.

The other items in the balance sheet are now analyzed and restated in terms of purchasing power as at the balance sheet date of December 31, 1974.

Marketable securities

	Historical	*Market value*
Bonds and debentures, at cost		
7% debentures redeemable in 1980 at 100	$ 200	$ 200
7½ % debentures redeemable in 1984 at 98, 1985 at 99, 1986 at 100	300	300
	$ 500	$ 500
X Company, acquired in 1966	568	500
Y Company, acquired in 1968	646	600
Z Company, acquired in 1970	156	150
MON Company, acquired in 1974	490	500
	$2,360	$2,250

The bonds and debentures are the same as those held at December 1973; these items are monetary and can be entered in the price-level column at the same amount as in the historical cost column, i.e. $500.

The other marketable securities held at December 1973 are still on hand. Normally their restated cost in December 1973 dollars would be converted by applying the conversion factor to arrive at their restated cost in 1974 dollars. In this case however, these marketable securities were carried in the 1973 GPL balance sheet at market value which was less than the GPL restated cost (see page 39). The conversion factor must be applied to the amount in the GPL balance sheet. This factor of 1.142 is applied therefore to the market value and not to the 1973 restated cost to arrive at the 1974 restated cost.

A new investment in MON Company was acquired in June 1974. This amount has to be restated from dollars of June 1974 purchasing power into dollars of December 1974 purchasing power. This is done by applying the conversion factor applicable to June 1974 which is 185/173, or 1.069.

	Cost	*Market value 1973 **	*Conversion factor*	*Price-level 1974 $*	*Market value 1974*
X Company	$ 568	$700	1.142	$ 799	$ 500
Y Company	646	725	1.142	828	600
Z Company	156	175	1.142	200	150
MON Company	490		1.069	524	500
	$1,860			$2,351	$1,750

*Substituted for 1973 restated cost; see discussion above.

The market value of these securities at December 1974 is $1,750; the historical cost is $1,860. As these are temporary investments, the carrying value in the historical cost accounts must be restricted to $1,750. This requires a provision for diminution in value of $110 which is charged in the income statement. In the GPL statements the cost of the investments on a restated 1974 dollar basis is $2,351. The same accounting principles are followed as in the historical cost statements and the carrying value of these investments is restricted to their market value of $1,750. This requires a provision for diminution of value in investments of $601, which is charged in the 1974 GPL income statement.

Inventories

Inventories in the historical cost balance sheet are analyzed as between raw materials, work in process and finished goods to ascertain when these costs were accumulated. Raw materials are carried on the first-in first-out basis and assumed to represent costs accumulated over the last four months of the year. Work in process is carried on the average cost basis and the costs have been accumulated over the last six months of the year. Finished goods are carried on the average cost basis and the costs have been accumulated over the last six months of the year. It is assumed that the depreciation included in the cost of overhead expenses is not sufficiently material to warrant separate analysis (see page 42).

Raw materials

$$\frac{\text{December 1974 month-end index}}{\text{Average of August to December 1974 month-end indices}}$$

$$= \frac{185}{(177 + 179 + 181 + 183 + 185) \div 5}$$

$$= \frac{185}{181} = 1.022$$

Work in process

$$\frac{\text{December 1974 month-end index}}{\text{Average June to December 1974 month-end indices}}$$

$$= \frac{185}{(173 + 175 + 177 + 179 + 181 + 183 + 185) \div 7}$$

$$= \frac{185}{179} = 1.034$$

Finished goods

$$\frac{\text{December 1974 month-end index}}{\text{Average June to December 1974 month-end indices}} = 1.034$$

The historical cost of inventories at December 31, 1974 can now be restated in December 1974 dollars.

	Historical	*Conversion factor*	*Price-level 1974 $*	*Net realizable value*
Raw materials	$29,450	1.022	$ 30,098	$28,550
Work in process	19,550	1.034	20,215	18,450
Finished goods	50,290	1.034	52,000	49,050
	$99,290		$102,313	$96,050

The restated inventory amounts are now compared with the net realizable value at December 31, 1974. In this case, the GPL amount exceeds net realizable value by $6,263 and a provision is made to reduce the inventories to the lower figure of $96,050.

In the historical statements a provision of $3,240 was necessary to reduce inventories to the lower of cost and net realizable value and has been included in cost of sales. It is debatable whether the provision on a price-level basis should also be included in the restated cost of sales figure for consistency, or grouped with other similar provisions that arise in the GPL statements. The matter is essentially one of presentation. The authors prefer using the same presentation in the GPL financial statements as in the historical cost statements.

As a provision to reduce inventories to net realizable value in the historical cost statements is included in cost of sales, so the similar provision in the GPL income statement is also included in cost of sales.

Prepaid expenses

Prepaid expenses in the December 1974 balance sheet are analyzed as follows:

Unexpired insurance	$320
Prepaid advertising	400
Prepaid interest	150
	$870

All of these prepaid expenses were incurred during the year 1974. The prepaid expenses which appeared in the December

1973 balance sheet have all been charged to the income statement during 1974. If any part of the December 1973 balance remained to be amortized after December 31, 1974, it would be updated to December 31, 1974 dollars. The analysis of prepaid expenses at December 1974 and the applicable conversion factors necessary to convert them into December 1974 dollars are illustrated below.

	1974	*Conversion factor*	*Price-level 1974 $*
April	$250	185/169 or 1.095	$274
September	500	185/179 or 1.034	517
December	120	185/185 or 1.000	120
	$870		$911

Investments in associated companies

The investment account at December 1974 is represented by:

Investment in DEF Ltd., at cost	$ 1,100
Investment in GHI Ltd., at equity	10,510
Advance to GHI Ltd.	1,500
	$13,110

There has been no change in the investment in DEF Ltd. The conversion factor of 1.142 is applied to the 1973 restated cost to arrive at the December 1974 restated cost.

	Price-level 1973 $	*Conversion factor*	*Price-level 1974 $*	*Market value*
Investment in DEF Ltd.	$1,650	1.142	$1,884	$1,200

Comparison of the 1974 restated amount and market value is considered on page 72.

No further advances have been made to GHI Ltd. during 1974, nor has any part of the advance been repaid. This advance is still considered to be in the nature of a long-term investment in GHI

Ltd., and is therefore still classified as a non-monetary item. Again, the conversion factor of 1.142 is applied to the 1973 restated cost to translate that amount into December 1974 purchasing power.

	Price-level 1973 $	*Conversion factor*	*Price-level 1974 $*
Advance to GHI Ltd.	$1,904	1.142	$2,174

The investment in GHI Ltd. which is carried on the equity basis cannot be restated simply by applying conversion factors to the amounts carried in the historical cost statements of this company. As discussed in relation to the restatement of the December 1973 balance sheet on page 44, it is essential to obtain the GPL statements of GHI Ltd. and to apply equity accounting to those statements. The transactions in the investment account between December 1973 and December 1974 are now analyzed and this must be done on both a historical basis and a GPL basis.

Investment in GHI Ltd.

	Historical cost		*Price-level*	
	Goodwill	*Net assets*	*Goodwill*	*Net assets*
Balance – December 31, 1973	$1,350	$ 8,610	$334	$11,150
Restated to December 31, 1974 dollars 185/162 or 1.142			382	12,733
40% interest in earnings of GHI Ltd.				
on historical basis		550		
on price-level basis				313
	$1,350	$ 9,160	$382	$13,046
		1,350		382
		$10,510		$13,428

The investments and advance can now be summarized as follows:

	Historical cost	*Price-level 1974 $*	*Market value*
DEF Ltd.	$ 1,100	$ 1,884	$ 1,200
GHI Ltd.	10,510	13,428	16,000
Advance to GHI Ltd.	1,500	2,174	–
	$13,110	$17,486	

Again it is necessary to compare historical cost and restated carrying value of the investments with market value at December 1974 to determine whether or not either exceeds market value and if so whether there is a permanent impairment of the investment.

The investment in GHI Ltd. has a market value which is higher than cost and restated cost of that investment and therefore no provision for impairment is necessary. The investment in DEF Ltd. has a historical cost of $1,100, a restated cost in December 1974 dollars of $1,884, and a market value of $1,200. In the historical cost statements the market value is higher than historical cost and no provision for impairment is necessary. However, in the GPL statements the market value is significantly below the carrying value.

This raises a general question whether there can be said to be impairment on the GPL basis when none is indicated on the historical cost basis. It might seem that if there were no impairment in the historical statements, recognition of an impairment in the GPL statements would represent a change in application of accounting principles. However, this is not a valid argument. In the historical cost statements the cost was compared with market to ascertain if there had been any diminution in value and there was none. The GPL statements follow the same accounting principles, but with the difference that restated cost is compared with market value to ascertain if there is any diminution in value on that basis. The writing down of an investment in the price-level statements from the restated cost to market value does not change the accounting principles but in fact follows those already established.

In preparing the 1973 GPL statements it was considered that there was no impairment in value. (See page 45.) Since 1973 the market value has declined and it is now assumed that the impairment in value is permanent. Although the comparison between cost and market value in the historical cost statements does not give rise to the necessity for a provision for impairment in value, the comparison of restated cost and market value in the GPL statements does indicate the necessity for such a provision for impairment of $684.

Investment in unconsolidated subsidiary

There have been no transactions affecting the investment in the subsidiary during the year. To obtain the restated cost of this investment in December 1974 dollars, the restated value in December 1973 dollars of $11,740 is updated by using the conversion factor of 1.142. The restated cost of the investment in the unconsolidated subsidiary is therefore $13,407 expressed in December 1974 dollars.

Property, plant and equipment

An analysis of the changes during the year in the property, plant and equipment accounts in the historical cost statements is shown below.

	December 31, 1973	*Additions*	*Retirements*	*December 31, 1974*
Cost				
Land	$ 6,560	$ –	$ –	$ 6,560
Buildings	$ 20,450	–	–	$ 20,450
Machinery and equipment	310,870	$30,250	$10,150	330,970
Furniture and fixtures	9,590	1,550	450	10,690
	$340,910	$31,800	$10,600	$362,110

	December 31, 1973	*Additions*	*Retirements*	*December 31, 1974*
Accumulated depreciation				
Buildings	$ 4,389	$ 511	$ –	$ 4,900
Machinery and equipment	104,236	16,528	8,775	111,989
Furniture and fixtures	4,665	1,069	439	5,295
	$113,290	$18,108	$ 9,214	$122,184

Retirements are reviewed to ascertain the years of acquisition. If the plant ledger is not sufficiently detailed to disclose this type of information, it may be necessary to use a method such as first-in first-out to estimate the year of acquisition of the assets which have been retired.

In this case it is assumed the machinery and equipment was originally acquired in the years 1954, 1956 and 1958 and the furniture and fixtures were originally acquired in the years 1964 and 1965. It is also necessary to ascertain the amount of accumulated depreciation related to these assets.

The analysis of the machinery and equipment account showing the historical cost and accumulated depreciation of the assets disposed of during the year and the additions made during 1974 follows.

	Historical cost	*Accumulated depreciation*
December 31, 1973 balances as previously analyzed	$310,870	$104,236
Less retirements		
Assets acquired		
1954	1,150	1,150
1956	4,250	3,825
1958	4,750	3,800
	$ 10,150	$ 8,775
	$300,720	$ 95,461
1974 – additions	30,250	
– depreciation at 5%		16,528
December 31, 1974 balances	$330,970	$111,989

The historical cost of machinery and equipment at December 31, 1974 is $330,970 but it can be determined from the summary on page 54 that $420 of this amount is represented by assets which are fully depreciated. Therefore depreciation is 5% of $330,550, which is $16,528.

The furniture and fixtures account is also analyzed to show the retirements during the year at their historical cost and related accumulated depreciation.

	Historical cost	*Accumulated depreciation*
December 31, 1973 balances as previously analyzed	$ 9,590	$4,665
Less retirements		
Assets acquired		
1964	340	340
1965	110	99
	$ 450	$ 439
	$ 9,140	$4,226
1974 – additions	1,550	
– depreciation at 10%		1,069
December 31, 1974 balances	$10,690	$5,295

When the property, plant and equipment accounts in the historical cost basis have been analyzed they can be translated to the GPL basis.

Land

There have been no transactions in land during this year, so the land as restated in the 1973 price-level balance sheet can be updated into 1974 dollars by applying the conversion factor of 1.142.

Price-level 1973 $	*Conversion factor*	*Price-level 1974 $*
$9,840	1.142	$11,237

Buildings

There have been no additions or retirements to the buildings during the current year. The balance in the buildings account at December 1973 expressed in 1973 dollars is restated to 1974 dollars by application of the conversion factor of 1.142. Depreciation is calculated on the cost outstanding at the beginning of each year; in the GPL statements it is calculated on the restated costs expressed in 1974 dollars. The balance of $30,198 in 1973 dollars is converted at 1.142, which amounts to $34,486 in 1974 dollars and depreciation for the year is calculated thereon. The analysis of the building account for 1974 is illustrated below:

	Restated cost	*Restated depreciation*
Balances at December 31, 1973 in 1973 $	$30,198	$6,503
No additions or retirements.		
Balances restated to 1974 $ at 1.142	$34,486	$7,426
Depreciation provided during year 2.5% of $34,486		862
Balances at December 31, 1974 in 1974 $	$34,486	$8,288

Machinery and equipment

The balance at December 31, 1973 expressed in 1973 dollars is converted into 1974 dollars by applying the conversion factor of 1.142.

During 1974 various items of machinery and equipment were disposed of either by sale or by scrapping. The cost and related depreciation for these items are expressed in 1974 dollars before being deducted from the asset and depreciation accounts. The items disposed of were originally acquired in 1954, 1956 and 1958. The conversion factors to restate these original costs into December 1973 dollars are shown in the analysis made of machinery and equipment in preparing the 1973 price-level balance sheet (see page 54). These original costs and the related accumulated depreciation, after restatement into December 1973 dollars, are translated into December 1974 dollars by application of the conversion factor of 1.142.

During 1974 various additions were made to the machinery and equipment. It is generally preferable to analyze the additions by months or quarters of acquisition and to apply the appropriate indices rather than the annual average.

The cost of the machinery and equipment restated into 1974 dollars is $494,096, before deducting fully depreciated assets. These assets were originally acquired in 1954 for $420 and were updated first into 1973 dollars and then into 1974 dollars; their restated amount was $863 which is deducted from the restated cost of $494,096 before calculating the depreciation. The depreciation for the year on machinery and equipment is $24,662.

		Restated cost	*Restated depreciation*
Balances at December 31, 1973 in 1973 $		$422,256	$152,510
Balances restated to 1974 $ by updating at 1.142		$482,216	$174,167
Retirements in 1974			
1954 Cost $1,150 × 1.800 × 1.142		2,364	
Depreciation $1,150 × 1.800 × 1.142			2,364
1956 Cost $4,250 × 1.742 × 1.142		8,455	
Depreciation $3,825 × 1.742 × 1.142			7,609
1958 Cost $4,750 × 1.688 × 1.142		9,157	
Depreciation $3,800 × 1.688 × 1.142			7,325
		$ 19,976	$ 17,298
		$462,240	$156,869
Additions in 1974			
April	$10,256 × 185/169 or 1.095	11,230	
July	5,489 × 185/175 or 1.057	5,802	
October	14,505 × 185/181 or 1.022	14,824	
	$30,250		
Depreciation 5% of $493,233 ($494,096 less $863)			24,662
Balances at December 31, 1974 in 1974 $		$494,096	$181,531

Furniture and fixtures

The balance at December 1973 expressed in 1973 dollars is updated into December 1974 dollars by application of the conversion factor of 1.142.

During the year various items included in the furniture and fixtures account were disposed of by sale or otherwise and these amounts are expressed in December 1974 dollars before being eliminated from the account. These items were acquired originally in 1964 and 1965. The conversion factors applicable to translate these amounts into December 1973 dollars are available from the analysis of furniture and fixtures account prepared at December 31, 1973. (See page 55.) These amounts are then updated into December 1974 dollars by application of the conversion factor of 1.142.

During the year 1974 various additions were made to this account. These additions have been analyzed into the appropriate month in which the cost was incurred and translated into December 1974 dollars by applying the appropriate conversion factor. Alternatively, the annual average index could be used in view of the relatively small amounts involved.

Depreciation on furniture and fixtures is calculated on a straight-line basis at the rate of 10% per annum on the cost of the items outstanding at the beginning of the year and acquired during the year, but is not calculated on any retirements. None of the items included in the furniture and fixtures account is fully depreciated so the depreciation for the year is 10% of the restated cost of furniture and fixtures expressed in December 1974 dollars.

		Restated cost	*Restated depreciation*
Balances at December 31, 1973 in 1973 $		$12,238	$6,324
Restated to 1974 $ by updating at 1.142		$13,976	$7,222
Retirement in 1974			
1964 Cost $340 × 1.558 × 1.142		605	
Depreciation $340 × 1.558 × 1.142			605
1965 Cost $110 × 1.500 × 1.142		188	
Depreciation $99 × 1.500 × 1.142			170
		$ 793	$ 775
		$13,183	$6,447
Additions in 1974			
February	$860 × 185/165 or 1.121	964	
October	690 × 185/181 or 1.022	705	
	$1,550		
Depreciation (10% of $14,852)			1,485
Balances at December 31, 1974 in 1974 $		$14,852	$7,932

Cost, accumulated depreciation and the 1974 provision for depreciation on both the historical and price-level bases can now be summarized in Figure 5.1.

Unamortized issue expense on long-term debt

The balance of issue expense outstanding at December 31, 1973 expressed in 1973 dollars is restated into its equivalent amount in December 1974 dollars by application of the conversion factor of 1.142. During 1974 part of this balance has been amortized into the income statement as the issue expense is being amortized over the 30 year life of the debentures. It is necessary to recalculate the amount of the amortization on a 1974 dollar basis. The balance at December 31, 1973 expressed in 1974 dollars, less the amortization during 1974 also expressed in 1974 dollars, gives the balance at December 31, 1974 on the price-level restated basis.

Figure 5.1

	Historical		*Price-level 1974 $*		*Provision for depreciation*	
	Cost	*Accumulated depreciation*	*Cost*	*Accumulated depreciation*	*Historical*	*Price-level 1974 $*
Buildings	$ 20,450	$ 4,900	$ 34,486	$ 8,288	$ 511	$ 862
Machinery and equipment	330,970	111,989	494,096	181,531	16,528	24,662
Furniture and fixtures	10,690	5,295	14,852	7,932	1,069	1,485
	$362,110	$122,184	$543,434	$197,751	$18,108	$27,009

	Historical	Price-level 1973 $	Price-level 1974 $
Issue expense in 1965	$620	$930	$1,062
Amortized to 1973	(186)	(279)	(318)
Balances at December 31, 1973	$434	$651	$ 744
1974 amortization			
– historical cost			
1/30 of $620	21		
– price-level			
1/30 of $1,062			35
Balances at December 31, 1974	$413		$ 709

Long-term debt

The analysis of the historical cost account for long-term debt at December 1974 shows the following amounts of debentures payable in local and in foreign currencies.

Sinking fund debentures class "A" due 1995		$22,079
Sinking fund debentures class "B" due 1995 (FC $28,200)		30,471
		$52,550
Less portion included in current liabilities		
Class "A" debentures	$172	
Class "B" debentures	198	
		370
		$52,180

When the debt was restated at December 31, 1973 the restated amount exceeded the local currency equivalent at the current rate of exchange and this latter amount was shown in the GPL statements. This becomes the starting point for the 1974 restatement calculation.

	1973 Local $	*Price-level Conversion factor*	*Restated 1974 Local $*
Long-term debt			
Current portion	$ 199	1.142	$ 227
Balance	28,082	1.142	32,070
	$28,281		$32,297
Payment in 1974 of 1973 current portion			227
			$32,070

Comparison at December 31, 1974 with local currency equivalent at current rate of exchange		
FC $ 200 at 0.9906	LC $198	
FC $28,000 at 0.9906	27,737	$27,935

As the liability when expressed in 1974 local dollars of $32,070 exceeds the local currency equivalent at the current rate of exchange of $27,935, the liability is restricted to the latter amount. The excess, which is the opposite of a provision for diminution in value, is credited to the price-level income statement.

1974 restated liability of FC $28,200	
– Liability in 1974 local dollars	$32,070
– Liability at current rate of exchange in 1974 local dollars	27,935
Price-level credit to income	$ 4,135

Share capital

There have been no transactions in the share capital account during the year and the redeemable preferred shares continue to be treated as a monetary item.

The amounts of the convertible preferred shares and the common shares are entered in the 1974 GPL balance sheet at the amount in the 1973 GPL balance sheet rolled forward to 1974 dollars by application of the conversion factor of 1.142.

	Historical	Price-level 1973 $	1974 $
Convertible preferred shares	$10,000	$ 15,730	$ 17,964
Common shares	$60,450	$128,356	$146,582

Excess of appraised value of fixed assets over cost

The restatement in 1973 of this historical balance indicated that the balance became a debit in the GPL statements and accordingly was offset against retained earnings (see page 58). There is thus no separate balance for this account in the GPL statements.

General price-level gain on preferred shares

During the year a price-level gain has accrued on the preferred shares which have been classified as monetary items (see page 37).

5% Redeemable preferred shares Historical, 1973 and 1974	$10,000
Price-level, 1973 in 1974 $	11,420
1974 in 1974 $	10,000
Price-level gain	$ 1,420

In this illustration the price-level gain on the preferred shares has been credited to a separate account in shareholders' equity. As mentioned on page 17, practice may vary on this point and in some countries the gain is credited in the GPL income statement. If this approach had been followed in the illustration, the amount of the gain would have been the same and hence net income for the year on the GPL basis would have been greater by $1,420.

Retained earnings

The retained earnings again represents the residual amount. In this case the amount will flow through from the 1974 statement of income and retained earnings when translated from a historical to a price-level basis.

A prior period adjustment included in historical statements must be analyzed to determine the date of origin of each part of the calculation that was used to arrive at the amount of the adjustment. Each part of the historical adjustment can then be restated by the appropriate conversion factor to arrive at the total of the prior period adjustment for price-level purposes.

Exhibit F

ABC Company
Balance Sheet
December 31, 1974

	Historical	*Price-level*	*Page reference*
ASSETS			
Current assets:			
Cash	$ 5,590	$ 5,590	*65*
Marketable securities	2,250	500	*65*
		1,750	*66*
Accounts receivable	61,580	61,580	*65*
Inventories	96,050	96,050	*68*
Prepaid expenses	870	911	*69*
	$166,340	$166,381	
Investments:			
In associated companies	13,110	1,200	*69*
		13,428	*70*
		2,174	*70*
In unconsolidated subsidiary	10,000	13,407	*72*
Fixed assets:			
Buildings, machinery and equipment	362,110	543,434	*79*
Less: Accumulated depreciation	(122,184)	(197,751)	*79*
Land	6,560	11,237	*74*
Other assets:			
Unamortized issue expense of long-term debt	413	709	*80*
	$436,349	$554,219	

Exhibit F (continued)

	Historical	*Price-level*	*Page reference*
LIABILITIES AND SHAREHOLDERS' EQUITY			
Current liabilities:			
Bank loan	$ 5,160	$ 5,160	65
Accounts payable	49,680	49,680	65
Income taxes	5,760	5,760	65
Current portion of long-term debt	370	370	80
	$ 60,970	$ 60,970	
Long-term debt	52,180	21,907	65
		27,737	81
Deferred income taxes	49,680	49,680	65
Shareholders' equity:			
Share capital	80,450	10,000	81
		17,964	82
		146,582	82
Price-level gain on preferred shares		1,420	82
Retained earnings	187,669	217,959	82
Excess of appraised value of assets over cost	5,400	—	82
	$436,349	$554,219	

6

Restating the Income Statement

The last of the four stages required for the preparation of GPL statements at December 31, 1974 by ABC Company is restating the 1974 historical income statement to dollars of December 31, 1974 purchasing power.

All items in the statement of income are restated for price-level changes by the same methods used to restate non-monetary assets and liabilities. In some cases the appropriate conversion factor can be applied to the balance of an income statement account; in others it may be necessary to analyze an account so that different conversion factors can be applied to its component parts. Practical considerations will also influence the amount of detail which it is necessary to determine in such analyses but in general terms and in the absence of marked seasonal variations most income statement items can be restated for GPL purposes using the average conversion factor for the year.

In companies where there are marked seasonal variations it may be necessary to use a weighted average price index, or perhaps to translate separately each quarter's transactions, or even each month's transactions. Items such as dividends and extraordinary items are converted by reference to the actual transaction dates and depreciation and amortization in the GPL income statement are computed by applying the rate of depreciation or amortization to the balance sheet accounts which have been restated into current year-end dollars.

The historical cost income statement for the year ended December 31, 1974 is shown as Exhibit G. The completed GPL income statement is shown as Exhibit H.

Sales

When sales revenue is assumed to have arisen evenly throughout the year, the conversion factor used is based on the average price-level for the year. The index at the end of 1974 is 185, the average index for the year is 174, and the average conversion factor for the year is 1.063. The rates at which sales are restated will affect the general price-level gain or loss. Sales involve the exchange of a non-monetary asset (inventories) for a monetary one (receivables or cash), and the loss from holding monetary assets begins to accrue from the date of the exchange. In this case, because sales revenue is assumed to have occurred evenly throughout the year, it is converted at the average conversion factor for the year.

Historical	*Conversion factor*	*Price-level 1974 $*
$427,745	1.063	$454,693

An illustration of how different conversion factors would be used for parts of the year in which disproportionate volumes of sales had been recorded was given on page 6.

Exhibit G

ABC Company
Statement of Income and Retained Earnings
For the year ended December 31, 1974

		Historical Cost Basis
Revenues:		
Sales		$427,745
Investment income		140
Gain on sale of fixed assets		650
		$428,535
Expenses:		
Cost of sales		260,510
Selling and administrative		98,340
Depreciation		18,108
Interest on long-term debt		4,221
		$381,179
Earnings before income taxes		$ 47,356
Income taxes:		
Current		17,368
Deferred		6,430
		$ 23,798
		$ 23,558
Provision to reduce investments to market value		110
		$ 23,448
Equity in earnings of associated company		550
Net income for year		$ 23,998
Retained earnings, beginning of year		179,784
		$203,782
Dividends:		
Preferred shares	$ 1,000	
Common shares	15,113	16,113
Retained earnings, end of year		$187,669
Earnings per share		$0.38

Investment income

The income from the investments is received from marketable securities which are carried on the cost basis. Assuming the income was received evenly throughout the year, it is converted at the average conversion factor for the year into December 1974 dollars.

Historical	*Conversion factor*	*Price-level 1974 $*
$140	1.063	$149

Gain on sale of fixed assets

The gain on sale of fixed assets must be recalculated by translating the proceeds of sale to dollars of 1974 purchasing power, and by comparing that amount with the depreciated cost of the assets retired, also expressed in dollars of 1974 purchasing power. The proceeds of sale on the historical basis, analyzed by month of disposal, and the original cost and accumulated depreciation of those assets retired are shown below.

Historical cost basis

	Cost	*Accumulated depreciation*	*Sales price*	*Profit (loss)*
Machinery and equipment	$10,150	$8,775	$2,031	$656
Furniture and fixtures	450	439	5	(6)
	$10,600	$9,214	$2,036	$650

Price-level basis

Proceeds of sales

The proceeds of sales analyzed by month are converted to December 1974 dollars by reference to the index applicable to the month of each sale.

Month of sale	*Sales Price*	*Conversion factor*	*Price-level 1974 $*
April	$ 250	185/169, or 1.095	$ 274
August	425	185/177, or 1.054	444
September	1,356	185/179, or 1.034	1,402
June	5	185/173, or 1.069	5
	$2,036		$2,125

Price-level cost of assets sold less accumulated depreciation

The restated cost and depreciation are shown in the analysis of fixed asset accounts (see pages 76 and 78). The price-level cost less related depreciation is $2,696 in 1974 dollars.

	Cost 1974 $	*Accumulated depreciation 1974 $*	*Net 1974 $*
Machinery and equipment	$19,976	$17,298	$2,678
Furniture and fixtures	793	775	18
	$20,769	$18,073	$2,696

Gain or loss on sales of fixed assets

In the historical statements, the disposals have resulted in a gain of $650. These calculations show that when the transactions are expressed in December 1974 dollars they resulted in fact in a loss on disposal in the GPL statements.

	Historical	*Price-level*
Proceeds of sales	$2,036	$2,125
Cost less accumulated depreciation	1,386	2,696
Gain (loss) on sales	$ 650	$ (571)

Cost of sales

The cost of sales on a historical basis is analyzed to show opening inventories, purchases and closing inventories. These amounts are then restated into December 1974 dollars. The restated amounts for the opening and closing inventories are obtained from the price-level balance sheets, that is, the 1973 price-level balance sheet rolled forward into December 1974 dollars and the 1974 price-level balance sheet (see pages 63 and 83). The purchases are assumed to have been made evenly throughout the year and are converted at the average conversion factor of 1.063.

	Historical	*Conversion factor*	*Price-level 1974 $*
Inventories at December 31, 1973	$ 98,560		$114,418
Purchases	258,000	1.063	274,254
	$356,560		$388,672
Inventories at December 31, 1974 before provision to reduce to net realizable value	99,290		102,313
	$257,270		$286,359
Reduction of inventories to net realizable value	3,240		6,263
	$260,510		$292,622

As discussed on page 68, the provision to reduce inventories to net realizable value on a price-level basis has been included in restated cost of sales and has not been shown separately in the restated income statement.

Selling and administrative expenses

The selling and administrative expenses are analyzed to segregate the part which relates to the amortization of prepaid expenses. The amount to be amortized on a price-level basis is the 1973 restated amount of $959 updated to December 1974 dollars by a conversion factor of 1.142. Although the expenses were amortized during 1974, this factor is not based on the 1974 average index because the charge against 1974 income has to be stated in terms of December 31, 1974 dollars. The write-off of prepaid expenses is therefore expressed in 1974 dollars at the amount derived from the analysis of the prepaid expenses in the 1973 balance sheet (see page 43).

The gain on translation of the current portion of the foreign currency debentures has not been shown separately in the income statement but has been included in selling and administrative expenses. These expenses are assumed to have accrued evenly during the year so again the average conversion factor of 1.063 is used to restate the expenses into December 1974 dollars.

	Historical	*Conversion factor*	*Price-level 1974 $*
Amortization of prepaid expenses	$ 940		$ 1,095
Other expenses	97,400	1.063	103,536
	$98,340		$104,631

Depreciation

The provisions for depreciation for the year on the buildings, machinery and equipment and furniture and fixtures are entered in the amounts previously calculated in the analysis of the fixed asset accounts in the balance sheet (see page 79).

	Historical	*Price-level 1974 $*
Buildings	$ 511	$ 862
Machinery and equipment	16,528	24,662
Furniture and fixtures	1,069	1,485
	$18,108	$27,009

It will be recognized that restating the depreciation provision on a price-level basis and rolling forward the accumulated depreciation in the GPL statements ensures that the restated asset cost is amortized over the same length of time in the GPL statements as in the historical statements.

In this example it has been assumed that depreciation has been provided on the straight-line method and the annual provision on a price-level basis has been calculated as a percentage of the restated cost of the fixed assets that were not fully depreciated.

(See page 76.) If historical depreciation had been provided on the reducing balance method, the annual provision on a price-level basis would also be calculated by reference to the restated cost of the fixed assets. A different approach is taken if historical depreciation is provided on the sinking fund method. In this case the historical provision comprises two elements—a fixed annual amount and interest compounded on the previously accumulated depreciation balance; for price-level restatement both elements of the provision are updated by a conversion factor which can be expressed as:

$$\frac{\text{Index at end of current year}}{\text{Index for month or quarter (or average for year) of acquisition of assets.}}$$

The balance of historical accumulated depreciation at the beginning of the year is rolled forward in the same manner as with accumulated depreciation calculated on other methods.

Interest on long-term debt

This account is analyzed to segregate the part relating to the amortization of issue expense on long-term debt. The amortization of the issue expense is expressed in 1974 dollars at the amount computed in the analysis of the balance sheet account (see page 80). The other interest expense is assumed to have accrued evenly during the year. If the expense did not accrue evenly it would be necessary to convert the amount by reference to the actual months or quarters in which the expense occurred; the date when the interest expense was paid is not of direct relevance in determining the conversion factor.

	Historical	*Conversion factor*	*Price-level 1974 $*
Amortization of issue expense	$ 21		$ 35
Other interest	4,200	1.063	4,465
	$4,221		$4,500

Income taxes

At present the taxation authorities in Canada, the United States and the United Kingdom, do not accept GPL accounting as a basis for preparing accounts for taxation purposes. Taxation liabilities are calculated by referring to income computed on the historical cost basis.

The question has been raised whether the provision for income taxes in GPL accounting should be based on the income taxes reflected in the historical cost statements or whether it should be based on the restated amounts.

In the United Kingdom, the Accounting Standards Steering Committee stated in Provisional SSAP No. 7:

> "Other matters that will need to be considered include . . . whether it may be necessary to include in the deferred tax account in the supplementary statement, an amount for the corporation tax . . . on any chargeable gain which would arise on a sale of the assets at the date of the balance sheet at the amount shown in the supplementary statement."

In the United States, the American Institute of Certified Public Accountants stated in APB Statement No. 3:

> "The Internal Revenue Code does not recognize general price-level restatements for tax purposes and income taxes are therefore assessed on the basis of historical-dollar amounts rather than amounts restated for general price-level changes. The income tax expense presented in general price-level statements is not computed in direct relationship to specific amounts of gains or losses on the statements or to the amount of net income before taxes. A few members of the Board believe that federal income tax should be allocated in general price-level statements to achieve a more direct relationship between the tax and various elements presented in these statements."

More recently, the Financial Accounting Standards Board in its exposure draft has stated:

"51. The amount of income tax expense included in determining net income in units of general purchasing power shall be based on the amount of income tax expense included in determining net income in units of money. No additional income taxes shall be accrued, either by a charge against general purchasing power net income or by a charge to stockholders' equity, for income taxes that may be paid in the future as a result of the non-deductibility for income tax purposes of the excess of amounts of nonmonetary assets stated in units of current general purchasing power over amounts of those assets stated in units of money."

"79. The Board concluded (paragraph 51) that no additional income taxes shall be accrued, either by a charge against general purchasing power net income or by a charge to stockholders' equity, for income taxes that may be paid as a result of the non-deductibility for income tax purposes of the excess of amounts of non-monetary assets stated in units of current general purchasing power over amounts of those assets stated in units of money. The basis for that conclusion is that restatement does not result in a "timing difference" as defined in APB Opinion No. 11, "Accounting for Income Taxes"—a difference between the periods in which a transaction affects taxable income and the periods in which it enters into pretax accounting income."

It has been suggested that tax allocation is necessary to ensure there is no overstatement of shareholders' equity in non-monetary assets. It has also been suggested that tax allocation should be recomputed on the timing differences between income for taxation purposes and income on the GPL income statement, that is, basically the difference between capital cost allowances and depreciation calculated on the restated cost of assets.

Counter arguments to tax allocation in GPL accounting are that the differences between historical cost taxable income and GPL accounting income are not "timing differences". GPL adjustments to non-monetary assets have no counterpart for income tax purposes and therefore represent "permanent differences". GPL adjustments to non-monetary assets are not credited to income statement; a provision for deferred taxes would therefore result in a mismatching of revenue and expenses in the income statement.

In the present circumstances, it is more appropriate that the income tax provision in the GPL income statement should be based on the income tax provision in the historical cost statements, expressed in dollars of end of year purchasing power. On the other hand, in the event that taxation authorities accepted GPL statements as a basis for the calculation of taxation liabilities, the provision for income taxes would be calculated accordingly and would involve a recomputation of deferred taxes.

In this illustration, income taxes for the year are assumed to have accrued evenly throughout the year, rather than to have accrued only at the balance sheet date (the present practice in the United Kingdom). The charge in the income statement is converted by the average conversion factor for the year of 1.063.

	Historical	*Conversion factor*	*Price-level 1974 $*
Current	$17,368	1.063	$18,462
Deferred	6,430	1.063	6,835
	$23,798		$25,297

Equity in earnings of associated company

The amount to be included is the share of the GPL earnings of the associated company GHI Ltd. which is obtained from the separate GPL statements of GHI Ltd. The reason for having separate GPL statements of the associated company was discussed on page 44. On page 70 ABC Company's share in the GPL earnings of the associated company for the year 1974 was shown as $313.

Provision to reduce to realizable values

Provisions to reduce assets to net realizable values are disclosed in the GPL income statement in the same way that similar provisions are disclosed in historical income statements. Thus, the provision to reduce inventories to net realizable value has been included in cost of sales (see page 90). Other provisions which were determined to be necessary relate to investments and are grouped for presentation in the income statement.

Provision to reduce investments to market values	
– marketable securities (see page 66)	$ 601
– investments in associated companies (see page 72)	684
	$1,285

Retained earnings

The opening retained earnings is the amount entered as the balancing figure in the 1973 GPL balance sheet ($195,267) now updated to 1974 dollars by application of the conversion factor of 1.142.

Price-level 1973 $	*Conversion factor*	*Price-level 1974 $*
$195,267	1.142	$222,995

Dividends

The dividends are analyzed by the various months or quarters in which they were declared and restated by application of the relevant conversion factor. When a proposed dividend is recorded at a year end in historical financial statements, the balance sheet item is monetary and is not restated. The amount charged against retained earnings is similarly not restated for GPL purposes.

		Historical	*Conversion factor*	*Price-level 1974 $*
Preferred shares				
May	$ 500		185/171, or 1.082	$ 541
October	500		185/181, or 1.022	511
		$ 1,000		
Common shares				
March	7,556		185/167, or 1.108	8,372
September	7,557	15,113	185/179, or 1.034	7,814
		$16,113		$17,238

General price-level gain or loss

The general purchasing power gain or loss is calculated by preparing a statement of source and application of net monetary items. This statement should list the monetary assets and liabilities on the historical basis at December 31, 1973 and 1974. The monetary items at December 31, 1973, rolled forward to their equivalents in 1974 dollars, are entered in the same schedule.

All items which caused a monetary inflow during the year are added in the statement of source and application of monetary items; these include sales, investment income and proceeds from sale of assets. From the total are deducted all items which caused a monetary outflow during the year; these include purchases, selling and administrative expenses, interest, income taxes, dividends, purchases of investments, prepaid expenses incurred and purchases of assets. Adding and deducting the amounts of monetary inflow and outflow during the year to and from the amount of the net monetary items at December 31, 1973 on the historical basis, gives the net monetary items on the historical basis at December 31, 1974. Each item is then shown at the amount restated to 1974 dollar values, as previously determined in the balance sheet and income statements, to arrive at net monetary items restated in December 31, 1974 dollars. This total reflects the individual transactions during the year and indicates what the net monetary items should have been worth at that date.

The statement shows net monetary liabilities at December 31, 1974 should have amounted to $73,714 but the actual net monetary liabilties amount only to $64,887. There has therefore been a gain in general purchasing power during the year in the amount of $8,827. As referred to on page 82 this amount does not include the price-level gain on preferred shares.

This amount is entered in the GPL income statement, allowing the completion of the statement of income and retained earnings which then shows a balance of retained earnings at the end of the year on the price-level basis in the amount of $217,959. It will be seen this amount corresponds with that already shown in the 1974 price-level balance sheet and the GPL financial statements are thereby completed.

Exhibit H

ABC Company
Statement of Income and Retained Earnings
For the year ended December 31, 1974

	Historical	*Price-level*	*Page reference*
Revenues:			
Sales	$427,745	$454,693	86
Investment income	140	149	88
Gain (loss) on sale of fixed assets	650	(571)	89
	$428,535	$454,271	
Expenses:			
Cost of sales	260,510	292,622	90
Selling and administrative	98,340	104,631	91
Depreciation	18,108	27,009	91
Interest on long-term debt	4,221	4,500	92
	$381,179	$428,762	
Earnings before income taxes	$ 47,356	$ 25,509	
Income taxes:			
Current	17,368	18,462	
Deferred	6,430	6,835	
	$ 23,798	$ 25,297	95
	$ 23,558	$ 212	
Provision to reduce investments to market value	110	—	
	$ 23,448	$ 212	
Equity in earnings of associated company	550	313	95
	$ 23,998	$ 525	
Price-level adjustments:			
General price-level gain		8,827	97
Foreign currency debt		4,135	81
Reduction of investments to market value		(1,285)	96
		$ 11,677	
Net income for year	$ 23,998	$ 12,202	
Retained earnings, beginning of year	179,784	222,995	96
	$203,782	$235,197	
Dividends	16,113	17,238	96
Retained earnings, end of year	$187,669	$217,959	

Exhibit I

ABC Company
Source and Application of Monetary Items

	Historical 1973	*Historical 1974*	*Historical 1973 in 1974 $*
Monetary items:			
Cash	$ 1,660	$ 5,590	$ 1,896
Marketable securities	500	500	571
Accounts receivable	63,480	61,580	72,494
	$ 65,640	$ 67,670	$ 74,961
Current liabilities	(62,250)	(60,970)	(71,089)
Debt	(22,079)	(21,907)	(25,214)
Deferred income taxes	(43,250)	(49,680)	(49,391)
	$ (61,939)	$ (64,887)	$ (70,733)

	Historical	*Restated 1974 $*
Net monetary items at December 31, 1973	$ (61,939)	$ (70,733)
Add: Monetary inflow—		
Sales	427,745	454,693
Investment income	140	149
Proceeds from sale of assets	2,036	2,125
	$429,921	$456,967
Deduct: Monetary outflow—		
Purchases	258,000	274,254
Selling and administrative expenses	97,400	103,536
Interest	4,200	4,465
Income taxes	23,798	25,297
Dividends	16,113	17,238
Purchase of marketable securities	490	524
Prepaid expenses incurred	870	911
Purchase of assets	31,800	33,525
	$432,671	$459,750
	$ (2,750)	$ (2,783)
Reclassification of current portion of class 'B' debentures	(198)	(198)
Decrease in monetary items during year	$ (2,948)	$ (2,981)
Restated, net monetary liabilities at December 31, 1974		$ (73,714)
Actual net monetary liabilities December 1974	$ (64,887)	(64,887)
General price-level gain		$ 8,827

7

The Application of Price-Level Accounting to Consolidated Financial Statements

Where a wholly-owned subsidiary has been incorporated by the parent company, no special problems arise in the preparation of GPL consolidated statements.

In these circumstances all the historical data relating to the subsidiary is available to the parent and the statements of the subsidiary can be readily consolidated with those of the parent before restatement for price-level purposes. GPL accounting can be applied to the historical consolidated statements in exactly the same way as it is applied to unconsolidated statements.

Where a subsidiary has been incorporated by the parent company but is not wholly-owned, separate GPL statements of the subsidiary are required to ensure that the minority interest on the GPL basis is correctly calculated. The calculation of minority interest is discussed in the Chapters 8 and 9 dealing with the acquisition of a subsidiary by purchase.

Unconsolidated financial statements were used in the previous chapters to illustrate the mechanics of GPL accounting. It will be remembered that the investment in the unconsolidated subsidiary, LMN Company Ltd. was carried at cost.

Having prepared its unconsolidated statements, the company will normally then prepare financial statements consolidated with those of its subsidiary for issue to its shareholders. The fundamental principles of price-level accounting that have already been described continue to govern the preparation of GPL consolidated statements. However, a number of problem areas are encountered in applying these principles on a consolidated basis depending upon the method of accounting used to reflect the acquisition of the subsidiary, that is, whether or not fair values were ascribed to the net assets of the subsidiary at the date of acquisition.

Bases of consolidation

For many years it was customary for the consolidated balance sheet to be prepared by adding the book values of the subsidiary's assets and liabilities to those of the parent, after eliminating intercompany transactions. Under this consolidation practice any difference between the cost of the investment in the subsidiary to the parent and the book value of the assets and liabilities of the subsidiary brought into the consolidation was classified as goodwill in the consolidated balance sheet.

More recently, the method of accounting used in preparing consolidated financial statements has been to ascribe fair values to the assets and liabilities of the subsidiary at the date of acquisition. Such values are not necessarily recorded in the books of the subsidiary, but on consolidation they are added to the book values of the parent company's assets and liabilities, again after eliminating any intercompany transactions. Any difference between the cost of the investment in the subsidiary to the parent and the fair values ascribed to the assets and liabilities of the subsidiary brought into the consolidation is classified as goodwill in the consolidated balance sheet.

GPL restatement of consolidated financial statements varies according to the consolidation practices adopted in the historical cost statements and on whether the subsidiary is wholly-owned. Basically the differences are that where a subsidiary is wholly-owned, separate price-level statements of the subsidiary are not required if the subsidiary is consolidated at fair values and are required only at the date of acquisition if the subsidiary is consolidated at book values; where the subsidiary is partly-owned separate price-level statements of the subsidiary are required at the date of acquisition and for subsequent years under either basis of consolidation.

The foregoing is summarized in Figure 7.1. The procedures for preparing GPL consolidated financial statements in relation to the two bases of consolidation are considered in Chapters 8 and 9.

Price-level statements of subsidiary at date of acquisition unavailable

Occasions may arise when GPL statements at the date of acquisition of a subsidiary cannot be prepared in the normal way. The subsidiary or subsidiaries may have been acquired many years previously and the effort involved in reconstructing the historical cost statements at that date in order to adjust to a price-level basis could be considerable.

The effort involved in reconstructing historical cost and GPL statements at the date of acquisition of each subsidiary must be weighed against the usefulness of the greater degree of accuracy that would be obtained in the GPL statements. In those cases where the effort involved in obtaining GPL statements of the subsidiary at the acquisition date is unwarranted, the best estimate possible should be made in order to calculate the goodwill on acquisition. This may involve working backwards from price-level statements at the current date; or in some cases, the goodwill arising in the historical cost statements at acquisition might be considered as equivalent to goodwill on a price-level basis. Judgment must be exercised according to the individual circumstances of each case.

Figure 7.1

Subsidiary incorporated by parent		*Subsidiary acquired by purchase*			
		Consolidated at book values		*Consolidated at fair values*	
Wholly-owned	*Partly-owned*	*Wholly-owned*	*Partly-owned*	*Wholly-owned*	*Partly-owned*
GPL statements not required.	GPL statements required.	GPL statements required only at date of acquisition.	GPL statements required.	GPL statements not required.	GPL statements required.
	Minority interest based on statements of subsidiary.		Minority interest based on statements of subsidiary.		Minority interest based on statements of subsidiary where fair values not allocated to minority interest.
					Minority interest based on statements of subsidiary as adjusted for fair values where fair values allocated to minority interest.
Goodwill – not applicable.	Goodwill – not applicable.	Goodwill recalculated at acquisition date.	Goodwill recalculated at acquisition date.	Goodwill in same amount as historical.	Goodwill in same amount as historical.

Pooling of interests

When a business combination has been accounted for as a pooling of interests, the assets and liabilities of the combining companies are merged at their respective book values in the historical balance sheet of the continuing company. This historical balance sheet can be restated for GPL purposes in the same manner as the balance sheet of any other single company. Thus, separate GPL statements of the individual companies included in a pooling of interests are not necessary.

8

Consolidation—Book Value Basis

When the book values of the subsidiary's assets and liabilities have been used in the historical consolidation, it is necessary to obtain GPL financial statements of the subsidiary for the preparation of price-level consolidated statements. GPL statements of the subsidiary are required at the date of acquisition and for each subsequent accounting period if the subsidiary is not wholly-owned.

GPL statements at the date of acquisition are required so that the actual cost of investment can be compared with the total restated amount of the net assets acquired, expressed in acquisition date dollars. Thus, if an acquisition had been made in 1970, the net assets acquired would be restated into 1970 dollars which would be compared with the actual cost of the acquisition. The difference arising from this comparison represents goodwill to the parent at the acquisition date, expressed in acquisition date dollars.

The goodwill calculated on this basis will probably be different from goodwill calculated on the historical cost basis. The purchase price of the subsidiary is the same under both bases but the amount of the net assets acquired, measured on the GPL basis, is different from the amount of net assets acquired, measured on the historical cost basis. This difference in the initial goodwill figure between the historical cost statements and the GPL statements will continue to exist but will not remain a constant amount.

GPL statements of the subsidiary for subsequent accounting periods are not required when the subsidiary is wholly-owned. In this case, the statements of the subsidiary can be consolidated with those of the parent and GPL accounting can then be applied to the consolidated financial statements. When the subsidiary is partly-owned, GPL statements of the subsidiary for subsequent accounting periods are required as the minority interest is calculated by reference to the separate price-level statements of the subsidiary. This in effect means the preparation of consolidated financial statements on the historical cost basis followed by a second consolidation on a GPL basis. The problems arising under this method are the elimination of intercompany transactions (which must be computed on a GPL basis in addition to the historical cost basis) and the treatment of goodwill and minority interest. These problems can be illustrated by an example of the preparation of consolidated financial statements.

ABC Company acquired its subsidiary, LMN Company Ltd., in December 1971; its condensed balance sheet at the date of acquisition is shown below.

	Historical	*Price-level 1971 $*	
Cash	$ 55	$ 55	
Receivables	1,105	1,105	
Inventories	1,490	1,512	(1)
Fixed assets (net)	9,338	11,463	(2)
	$11,988	$14,135	
Current liabilities	$ 1,650	$ 1,650	
Shareholders' equity			
Share capital	8,000	10,224	(3)
Retained earnings	2,338	2,261	
	$11,988	$14,135	

(1) For purposes of this illustration:
   (a) the inventories are assumed to represent three months accumulation of costs,
   (b) an average index for the period October, November, December 1971 of 136 has been used, and
   (c) the index at the end of December 1971 was 138.

Inventories expressed in December 1971 dollars are therefore:

$1,490 × 138/136, or 1.015 = $1,512

(2) An analysis of fixed asset costs and years of purchase is shown below, with straight-line depreciation over 40 years on 1965 additions totalling $3,500 and over 20 years on all other additions. Indices applicable to the fixed asset additions are as follows:

	Average	*Year-end*
1965	108	Not required
1968	122	Not required
1971	Not required	138

				Price-level 1971 $	
	Cost	*Accumulated depreciation*	*Conversion factor*	*Cost*	*Accumulated depreciation*
1965	$ 3,500	$ 612	138/108, or 1.278	$ 4,473	$ 782
1965	5,000	1,750	138/108, or 1.278	6,390	2,237
1968	4,000	800	138/122, or 1.131	4,524	905
	$12,500	$3,162		$15,387	$3,924
Net book value		$9,338		$11,463	

(3) The share capital is assumed to consist of common shares, issued in 1965.

$8,000 × 138/108, or 1.278 = $10,224

The historical and GPL statements of LMN Company Ltd. for each year subsequent to its acquisition by ABC Company are shown on pages 108 and 109. Calculations to arrive at GPL restatements for each year follow these summarized statements.

Indices used in the GPL restatements are as follows:

	1971	*1972*	*1973*	*1974*
June	–	–	–	173
Average, October to December	–	143	161	182
December	138	150	162	185
Average for year	–	142	156	174

Balance Sheet

	1972		*1973*		*1974*	
	Historical	*Price-level 1972 $*	*Historical*	*Price-level 1973 $*	*Historical*	*Price-level 1974 $*
Cash	$ 1,015	$ 1,015	$ 1,930	$ 1,930	$ 2,942	$ 2,942
Receivables	1,655	1,655	2,405	2,405	2,050	2,050
Receivable from parent					600	600
Inventories	1,590	1,668	1,650	1,660	1,750	1,778
Fixed assets	12,500	16,726	12,500	18,064	14,000	22,232
Accumulated depreciation	(3,699)	(4,980)	(4,236)	(6,150)	(4,848)	(7,984)
	$13,061	$16,084	$14,249	$17,909	$16,494	$21,618
Liabilities	$ 1,472	$ 1,472	$ 1,480	$ 1,480	$ 2,730	$ 2,730
Share capital	8,000	11,113	8,000	12,003	8,000	13,707
Retained earnings	3,589	3,499	4,769	4,426	5,764	5,181
	$13,061	$16,084	$14,249	$17,909	$16,494	$21,618

Income statement and retained earnings

	1972		*1973*		*1974*	
	His-torical	*Price-level 1972 $*	*His-torical*	*Price-level 1973 $*	*His-torical*	*Price-level 1974 $*
Revenue	$9,600	$10,138	$9,700	$10,069	$9,900	$10,524
Cost of sales	3,962	4,264	4,163	4,524	4,463	4,968
Depreciation	537	714	537	772	612	961
Expenses	2,600	2,746	2,650	2,751	2,850	3,030
	$7,099	$ 7,724	$7,350	$ 8,047	$7,925	$ 8,959
	$2,501	$ 2,414	$2,350	$ 2,022	$1,975	$ 1,565
Price-level loss		53		160		396
Income taxes	1,250	1,320	1,170	1,214	980	1,042
Net income	$1,251	$ 1,041	$1,180	$ 648	$ 995	$ 127
Retained earnings	2,338	2,458	3,589	3,778	4,769	5,054
Retained earnings	$3,589	$ 3,499	$4,769	$ 4,426	$5,764	$ 5,181

Calculations for LMN Company Ltd. GPL statements, 1972 to 1974

1. *Inventories*

Assumed to represent three months accumulation of costs each year

	1972	*1973*	*1974*
Conversion factors	150/143 or 1.049	162/161 or 1.006	185/182 or 1.016
Historical	$1,590	$1,650	$1,750
Price-level	$1,668	$1,660	$1,778

2. *Fixed assets*

		1972	*1973*	*1974*
Conversion factors		150/138 or 1.087	162/150 or 1.080	185/162 or 1.142
1971				
Historical	*Price-level*			
$ 3,500	$ 4,473	$ 4,862	$ 5,251	$ 5,996
5,000	6,390	6,946	7,502	8,567
4,000	4,524	4,918	5,311	6,065
$12,500	$15,387	$16,726	$18,064	$20,628
1,500*	–	–	–	1,604
$14,000	$15,387	$16,726	$18,064	$22,232

*June 1974 purchase. Conversion factor to update to December 31, 1974 185/173, or 1.069

3. *Accumulated depreciation*

The accumulated depreciation in 1971 dollars was $3,924 (see page 107) which is restated in 1972 dollars at 1.087		$4,266
Add: Depreciation provision, 1972		
2½% of $4,862	$ 121	
5% of $6,946	347	
5% of $4,918	246	714
		$4,980
$4,980 restated in 1973 dollars at 1.080		$5,378
Add: Depreciation provision, 1973		
2½% of $5,251	$ 131	
5% of $7,502	375	
5% of $5,311	266	772
		$6,150
$6,150 restated in 1974 dollars at 1.142		$7,023
Add: Depreciation provision, 1974		
2½% of $5,996	$ 150	
5% of $8,567	428	
5% of $6,065	303	
5% of $1,604	80	961
		$7,984

The amounts on which the depreciation provisions are calculated are taken from calculation 2. Fixed assets above.

4. *Share capital*

Historical	$ 8,000
Price-level in 1971 dollars (page 107)	$10,224
Restated in 1972 dollars at 1.087	$11,113
Restated in 1973 dollars at 1.080	$12,003
Restated in 1974 dollars at 1.142	$13,707

5. *Revenue*

Assumed to have accrued evenly throughout each year.

	1972	*1973*	*1974*
Conversion factors	150/142 or 1.056	162/156 or 1.038	185/174 or 1.063
Historical	$ 9,600	$ 9,700	$ 9,900
Price-level	$10,138	$10,069	$10,524

6. *Cost of sales*

	1972		*1973*		*1974*	
	His-torical	*Price-level*	*His-torical*	*Price-level*	*His-torical*	*Price-level*
Opening inventories	$1,490	$1,643 (1)	$1,590	$1,801 (4)	$1,650	$1,896 (5)
Purchases	4,062	4,289 (2)	4,223	4,383 (2)	4,563	4,850 (2)
	$5,552	$5,932	$5,813	$6,184	$6,213	$6,746
Closing inventories	1,590	1,668 (3)	1,650	1,660 (3)	1,750	1,778 (3)
Cost of sales	$3,962	$4,264	$4,163	$4,524	$4,463	$4,968

(1) Inventories in 1971 GPL balance sheet of $1,512 restated to 1972 dollars; conversion factor – 1.087.

(2) Assumed to have accrued evenly throughout each year

1972 = $4,062 × 1.056 = $4,289
1973 = $4,223 × 1.038 = $4,383
1974 = $4,563 × 1.063 = $4,850

(3) From closing balance sheets.

(4) Inventories in 1972 GPL balance sheet of $1,668 restated to 1973 dollars; conversion factor – 1.080.

(5) Inventories in 1973 GPL balance sheet of $1,660 restated to 1974 dollars; conversion factor – 1.142.

7. *Depreciation on historical cost basis*

Annual charge	*1972 and 1973*	*1974*
2½% of $3,500	$ 87	$ 87
5% of $5,000	250	250
5% of $4,000	200	200
5% of $1,500	—	75
	$537	$612

8. *Expenses*

Assumed to have accrued evenly throughout each year.

	1972	*1973*	*1974*
Conversion factors	150/142 or 1.056	162/156 or 1.038	185/174 or 1.063
Historical	$ 2,600	$ 2,650	$ 2,850
Price-level	$ 2,746	$ 2,751	$ 3,030

9. *General price-level gain or loss*

Source and application of monetary items.

	1971		*1972*		*1973*		*1974*
	Historical	*In 1972 $*	*Historical*	*In 1973 $*	*Historical*	*In 1974 $*	*Historical*
Cash	$ 55	$ 60	$1,015	$1,096	$1,930	$2,204	$2,942
Receivables	1,105	1,201	1,655	1,788	2,405	2,746	2,650
Liabilities	(1,650)	(1,793)	(1,472)	(1,590)	(1,480)	(1,690)	(2,730)
	$ (490)	$ (532)	$1,198	$1,294	$2,855	$3,260	$2,862

	1972		*1973*		*1974*	
	Historical	*Price-Level*	*Historical*	*Price-Level*	*Historical*	*Price-Level*
Opening monetary item	$ (490)	$ (532)	$1,198	$ 1,294	$2,855	$ 3,260
Sales	$9,600	$10,138	$9,700	$10,069	$9,900	$10,524
Purchases	$4,062	$ 4,289	$4,223	$ 4,383	$4,563	$ 4,850
Expenses	2,600	2,746	2,650	2,751	2,850	3,030
Purchase of fixed assets					1,500	1,604
Income taxes	1,250	1,320	1,170	1,214	980	1,042
	$7,912	$ 8,355	$8,043	$ 8,348	$9,893	$10,526

	1972		*1973*		*1974*	
	Historical	*Price-Level*	*Historical*	*Price-Level*	*Historical*	*Price-Level*
Increase (decrease) in monetary items	$1,688	$ 1,783	$1,657	$ 1,721	$ 7	$ (2)
Closing monetary items	1,198	1,251	2,855	3,015	2,862	3,258
Actual net monetary items	$1,198	$ 1,198	$2,855	$ 2,855	$2,862	$ 2,862
Price-level loss		$ 53		$ 160		$ 396

10. *Income taxes*

Assumed to have accrued evenly throughout each year.

	1972	*1973*	*1974*
Conversion factors	150/142 or 1.056	165/156 or 1.038	185/174 or 1.063
Historical	$1,250	$1,170	$ 980
Price-level	$1,320	$1,214	$1,042

11. *Retained earnings*

1971 GPL balance sheet updated to 1972—$2,261 at 1.087	$2,458
1972 GPL balance sheet updated to 1973—$3,499 at 1.080	$3,778
1973 GPL balance sheet updated to 1974—$4,426 at 1.142	$5,054

Calculation of goodwill on acquisition

To calculate goodwill at the date of acquisition, it is necessary to obtain the GPL financial statements of the subsidiary at that date and compare the actual cost of acquisition with the price-level restated cost of the net assets acquired, expressed in acquisition date dollars.

ABC Company acquired LMN Company Ltd. in December 1971 at a cost of $10,000. The condensed balance sheets of LMN Company Ltd. at the date of acquisition (see page 106) showed:

Net assets on historical cost basis, i.e. carrying values in historical statements of LMN Company Ltd.	$10,338
Net assets in GPL statements of LMN Company Ltd.	$12,485

Assuming ABC Company had purchased 75% of the shares of LMN Company Ltd., the goodwill resulting from the acquisition would be:

	Historical	*Price-level 1971 $*
Purchase price	$10,000	$10,000
Net assets acquired (75% of total net assets)	7,753	9,364
	$ 2,247	$ 636

In the GPL consolidated balance sheet the amount to be shown as goodwill at date of acquisition is $636. This amount is classified as non-monetary and is updated in the GPL consolidated balance sheet.

Subsequent treatment of goodwill

The accounting treatment of goodwill acquired in 1971 may have followed one of three practices that were acceptable at that time.

1. Goodwill may have been written off to retained earnings at the date of acquisition.
2. Goodwill may have been carried in the balance sheet at original cost.
3. Goodwill may have been carried in the balance sheet at cost and subsequently amortized.

It should be noted that since 1971 official pronouncements of professional accountancy bodies in some countries have made mandatory the amortization of goodwill arising from business combinations and no longer allow goodwill to be written off to retained earnings at the date of the combination or to be carried indefinitely as an asset. These pronouncements do not have retroactive effect however and it therefore remains necessary for GPL accounting purposes to determine the practice that was followed in the historical statements when goodwill arose.

1. *Goodwill written off to retained earnings*

If the goodwill on acquisition had been written off to retained earnings in the year of acquisition, the entries in the consolidated historical and GPL statements would be:

	Historical	*Price-level 1971 $*
Retained earnings at December 1971	$xxx,xxx	$xxx,xxx
Less write off of goodwill on acquisition of subsidiary	2,247	636
Retained earnings at December 1971	$xxx,xxx	$xxx,xxx

2. *Goodwill carried on balance sheet at original cost*

If the goodwill on acquisition has been retained in the balance sheet at original cost, it would be reflected in the consolidated historical and GPL statements in the following manner:

	Historical	*Price-level*
Goodwill, at cost		
December 1971 Balance sheet	$2,247	$ 636
December 1972 Balance sheet	$2,247	
updated to 1972 dollars 150/138 or 1.087		$ 691
December 1973 Balance sheet	$2,247	
updated to 1973 dollars 162/150 or 1.080		$ 746
December 1974 Balance sheet	$2,247	
updated to 1974 dollars 185/162 or 1.142		$ 852

3. *Goodwill carried on balance sheet at cost less amortization*

If the goodwill has been amortized over an estimated life of, say, 30 years, it would be reflected in the consolidated historical and GPL statements as follows.

	Historical basis	Price-level basis Cost	Amortiz-ation	Net
December 1971 Balance sheet	$2,247	$636		
December 1972				
Updated to 1972 dollars		691		
Less amortization				
1/30 of $2,247	75			
1/30 of $ 691			23	
Balance sheet amount	$2,172	$691	$23	$668
December 1973				
Updated to 1973 dollars		746	25	721
Less amortization				
1/30 of $2,247	75			
1/30 of $ 746			25	25
Balance sheet amount	$2,097	$746	$50	$696
December 1974				
Updated to 1974 dollars		852	57	795
Less amortization				
1/30 of $2,247	75			
1/30 of $ 852			28	28
Balance sheet amount	$2,022	$852	$85	$767

The charge for amortization on the historical cost basis is the same amount each year. On the GPL basis, however, the original amount of $636 is restated each year in dollars of purchasing power at that year-end and the amortization charge is based on that restated amount.

If during the 30 year period the goodwill became permanently impaired and the unamortized historical balance were written off, the amount written off in the GPL statements would be the unamortized restated balance at the beginning of the year in which the write-off was made, rolled forward to dollars of value at the end of that year.

Negative goodwill

If the acquisition of the subsidiary had resulted in "negative goodwill" in the consolidated historical cost statements and also in negative goodwill in the GPL consolidated statements, the accounting for the negative goodwill in the price-level statements would have been the same as that in the historical cost statements. It could happen that an acquisition resulted in historical goodwill which, when translated to a price-level basis, became negative goodwill. In other words, restatement of the acquisition transaction has resulted in a negative amount for price-level purposes which must be accounted for on the same basis as has been adopted for positive goodwill in the historical financial statements.

Negative goodwill is sometimes disclosed as a separate part of shareholders' equity and carried at original acquisition amount. In Canada and the United States official pronouncements no longer permit this treatment, except where the negative goodwill arose on a business combination before the effective dates of the respective pronouncements; any such amounts are reflected in the fair values ascribed to assets acquired in the business combination and cannot be separately disclosed.

Calculation of minority interest on acquisition

ABC Company has purchased 75% of the shares of LMN Company Ltd. The minority interest at date of acquisition on the historical and GPL basis is calculated in the following manner:

	Historical	*Price-level 1971 $*
Total net assets of LMN Company Ltd.	$10,338	$12,485
Less 75% acquired by ABC Company	7,753	9,364
Minority interest	$ 2,585	$ 3,121

In the GPL consolidated statements of subsequent years the minority interest, calculated on the price-level basis, is updated to dollars of purchasing power at each balance sheet date. The minority interest's share of the earnings of LMN Company Ltd., calculated from the GPL income statement of LMN Company Ltd., (see page 109) is added to the restated amount each year as shown below.

	Historical	*Price-level*
Minority interest at acquisition	$2,585	$3,121
1972 – Updated to 1972 dollars at 1.087		$3,393
Share of earnings		
25% of $1,251	313	
25% of $1,041		260
	$2,898	$3,653
1973 – Updated to 1973 dollars at 1.080		$3,945
Share of earnings		
25% of $1,180	295	
25% of $ 648		162
	$3,193	$4,107
1974 – Updated to 1974 dollars at 1.142		$4,690
Share of earnings		
25% of $995	248	
25% of $127		32
	$3,441	$4,722

The minority interest can also be calculated from the balance sheet of the subsidiary in the same way as in the original calculation of the minority interest at date of acquisition.

	Historical	*Price-level 1974 $*
Total net assets of LMN Company Ltd. at December 1974 in balance sheet of LMN Company Ltd.	$13,764	$18,888
Minority interest therein, 25%	$ 3,441	$ 4,722

Consolidation procedures subsequent to acquisition date

When the amounts for goodwill and minority interest have been restated on a GPL basis, the consolidation procedures for GPL statements are the same as those for historical cost statements. Any intercompany transactions eliminated in the preparation of historical cost consolidated statements are expressed on a price-level basis and eliminated in the GPL consolidated statements.

Intercompany transactions

Assumptions:

1. In 1974, the subsidiary, LMN Company Ltd. sold goods to its parent company for a total of $2,000; $1,000 of these goods remained in the parent company's inventory at December 31, 1974. LMN Company Ltd. had a 25% gross profit margin on these goods.
2. At December 31, 1974, ABC Company had, included in its accounts payable, an outstanding payable to the subsidiary of $600.
3. During June 1974, ABC Company sold to LMN Company Ltd., fixed assets of its own manufacture for $1,500. The cost of manufacture of these assets was $1,250.

Consolidating adjustments—historical cost basis

The work sheet for the consolidating adjustments at date of acquisition and for 1972 to 1974, is set out in Exhibit J. Intercompany eliminations are dealt with separately on Exhibit K simply for clarity in the illustration.

Exhibit J

ABC Company
Consolidated Work Sheet

Historical Cost Basis
December 31, 1974

	Parent	*Subsidiary*	*Consolidating Entries* *Dr.*	*Consolidating Entries* *Cr.*	*Consolidated Total Prior to 1974 Intercompany Eliminations*
Inventories	$ 96,050	$ 1,750			$ 97,800
Receivable from parent		600			600
Other current assets	70,290	4,992			75,282
Investments	23,110			$10,000 (1)	13,110
Fixed assets	246,486	9,152			255,638
Other assets	413				413
Goodwill			$ 2,247 (3)		2,247
	$436,349	$16,494			$445,090
Payable to subsidiary	$ 600				$ 600
Other current liabilities	60,370	$ 2,730			63,100
Long-term debt	52,180				52,180
Deferred taxes	49,680				49,680
Share capital	80,450	8,000	8,000 (2)		80,450
Retained earnings	187,669	5,764	3,194 (5)		190,239
Appraisal credit	5,400				5,400
Minority interest				3,441 (4)	3,441
	$436,349	$16,494			$445,090

	Parent	Subsidiary	Consolidating Entries Dr.	Consolidating Entries Cr.	Consolidated Total Prior to 1974 Intercompany Eliminations
Sales	$427,745	$ 9,900			$437,645
Other income	790				790
	$428,535	$ 9,900			$438,435
Cost of sales	$260,510	$ 4,463			$264,973
Selling and administrative	98,340	2,850			101,190
Depreciation	18,108	612			18,720
Interest	4,221				4,221
	$381,179	$ 7,925			$389,104
	$ 47,356	$ 1,975			$ 49,331
Income taxes	23,798	980			24,778
	$ 23,558	$ 995			$ 24,553
Provisions	(110)				(110)
Equity interest	550				550
	$ 23,998	$ 995			$ 24,993
Minority interest			248 (6)		248
Net income	$ 23,998	$ 995			$ 24,745
Retained earnings	179,784	4,769	3,194 (5)	248 (6)	181,607
	$203,782	$ 5,764			$206,352
Dividends	16,113				16,113
Retained earnings	$187,669	$ 5,764			$190,239

Consolidating entries

(1) The elimination of the investment in the subsidiary carried in the parent's books at a cost of $10,000.

(2) The elimination of the subsidiary's share capital in the amount of $8,000.

(3) The setting up of goodwill on acquisition of $2,247 which is carried in the consolidated balance sheet at cost.

(4) The setting up of minority interest at original amount at acquisition date plus share of earnings to date, which amount is $3,441 being equivalent to 25% of the net assets of $13,764 of the subsidiary at December 1974.

(5) The removal from retained earnings of pre-acquisition profits and minority interest in subsequent earnings.

Retained earnings of subsidiary at date of acquisition		$2,338
Minority interest in earnings		
	1972 – $313	
	1973 – $295	
	1974 – $248	856
		$3,194

(6) The setting up of minority interest in 1974 earnings in the amount of $248.

Intercompany eliminations

The work sheet showing intercompany eliminations for the year 1974 is shown as Exhibit K. For convenience of illustration, the effect of income taxes on the intercompany transactions has been ignored.

Exhibit K

ABC Company
Consolidated Work Sheet
Historical Cost Basis
December 31, 1974

	Consolidated Total Prior to 1974 Intercompany Eliminations	*1974 Intercompany Eliminations Dr.*	*Cr.*	*Consolidated Total*
Inventories	$ 97,800		$ 250 (2)	$ 97,550
Receivable from parent	600		600 (3)	—
Other current assets	75,282			75,282
Investments	13,110			13,110
Fixed assets	255,638	$ 13 (5)	250 (4)	255,401
Other assets	413			413
Goodwill	2,247			2,247
	$445,090			$444,003
Payable to subsidiary	$ 600	600 (3)		
Other current liabilities	63,100			$ 63,100
Long-term debt	52,180			52,180
Deferred taxes	49,680			49,680
Share capital	80,450			80,450
Retained earnings	190,239	250 (4)	13 (5)	189,752
		250 (2)		
Appraisal credit	5,400			5,400
Minority interest	3,441			3,441
	$445,090			$444,003

Exhibit K (continued)

	Consolidated Total Prior to 1974 Intercompany Eliminations	*1974 Intercompany Eliminations*		*Consolidated Total*
		Dr.	*Cr.*	
Sales	$437,645			$435,395
		250 (4)		
		2,000 (1)		
Other income	790			790
	$438,435			$436,185
Cost of sales	$264,973	250 (2)	2,000 (1)	$263,223
Selling and administrative	101,190			101,190
Depreciation	18,720		13 (5)	18,707
Interest	4,221			4,221
	$389,104			$387,341
	$ 49,331			$ 48,844
Income taxes	24,778			24,778
	$ 24,553			$ 24,066
Provisions	(110)			(110)
Equity interest	550			550
	$ 24,993			$ 24,506
Minority interest	248			248
Net income	$ 24,745			$ 24,258
Retained earnings	181,607			181,607
	$206,352			$205,865
Dividends	16,113			16,113
		250 (2)	13 (5)	
Retained earnings	$190,239	250 (4)		$189,752

Intercompany eliminations

(1) The elimination of intercompany sale of goods of $2,000.

(2) The elimination of intercompany profits on inventories acquired by the parent from the subsidiary, i.e. 25% of $1,000.

(3) The elimination of the intercompany accounts payable and receivable.

(4) The elimination of intercompany profits on the sale of fixed assets by the parent to the subsidiary, i.e. $250.

(5) The adjustment of depreciation as a result of (4) above, i.e. 5% on $250.

The net amount of fixed assets is arrived at as follows:

	Cost	*Accumulated depreciation*	*Net*
Land	$ 6,560	—	$ 6,560
Other fixed assets			
Parent	$362,110	$122,184	
Subsidiary	14,000	4,848	
	$376,110	$127,032	
Intercompany elimination	250	13	
	$375,860	$127,019	248,841
			$255,401

Consolidating adjustments—price-level basis

The work sheet for the consolidating adjustments at date of acquisition and for 1972 to 1974 on a GPL basis is shown as Exhibit L.

Exhibit L

ABC Company
Consolidated Work Sheet
General Price-Level Basis
December 31, 1974

	Parent	Subsidiary	Consolidating Entries Dr.	Consolidating Entries Cr.	Consolidated Total Prior to 1974 Intercompany Eliminations
Inventories	$ 96,050	$ 1,778			$ 97,828
Receivable from parent		600			600
Other current assets	70,331	4,992			75,323
Investments	30,209			$13,407 (1)	16,802
Fixed assets	356,920	14,248			371,168
Other assets	709				709
Goodwill			$ 852 (3)		852
	$554,219	$21,618			$563,282
Payable to subsidiary	$ 600				$ 600
Other current liabilities	60,370	$ 2,730			63,100
Long-term debt	49,644				49,644
Deferred taxes	49,680				49,680
Share capital	174,546	13,707	13,707 (2)		174,546
Retained earnings	217,959	5,181	3,570 (5)		219,570
Price-level gain	1,420				1,420
Minority interest				4,722 (4)	4,722
	$554,219	$21,618			$563,282

	Parent	Subsidiary	Consolidating Entries Dr.	Consolidating Entries Cr.	Consolidated Total Prior to 1974 Intercompany Eliminations
Sales	$454,693	$10,524			$465,217
Other income	(422)				(422)
	$454,271	$10,524			$464,795
Cost of sales	$292,622	$ 4,968			$297,590
Selling and administrative	104,631	3,030			107,661
Depreciation	27,009	961			27,970
Interest	4,500				4,500
	$428,762	$ 8,959			$437,721
	$ 25,509	$ 1,565			$ 27,074
Income taxes	25,297	1,042			26,339
	$ 212	$ 523			$ 735
Equity interest	313				313
Price-level gain (loss)	12,962	(396)			12,566
	$ 13,487	$ 127			$ 13,614
Provisions	1,285				1,285
	$ 12,202	$ 127			$ 12,329
Minority interest			32 (6)		32
Net income	12.202	127			$ 12,297
Retained earnings	222,995	5,054	3,570 (5)	32 (6)	224,511
	$235,197	$ 5,181			$236,808
Dividends	17,238				17,238
Retained earnings	$217,959	$ 5,181			$219,570

Consolidating entries

(1) The elimination of the investment in the subsidiary, carried in the parent's GPL statements at restated cost in 1974 dollars of $13,407.

(2) The elimination of the subsidiary's share capital in the restated amount of $13,707.

(3) The setting up of goodwill on acquisition of $636 in 1971 dollars restated to $852 in 1974 dollars.

(4) The setting up of minority interest at its original amount at acquisition date plus share of earnings to date, all expressed in 1974 dollars, which amount is $4,722 being equivalent to 25% of the net assets of $18,888 in the GPL balance sheet of the subsidiary at December 31, 1974.

(5) The removal from retained earnings of pre-acquisition profits and minority interest in subsequent earnings.

Retained earnings of subsidiary at date of acquisition, in 1971 dollars	$2,261	
equivalent in 1972 dollars, at 1.087	$2,458	
equivalent in 1973 dollars, at 1.080	$2,655	
equivalent in 1974 dollars, at 1.142		$3,032
Minority interest in earnings, expressed in 1974 dollars		
1972 – $260 × 1.080 × 1.142	$321	
1973 – $162 × 1.142	185	
1974 – $ 32	32	538
		$3,570

(6) The setting up of minority interest in the restated amount of $32.

Intercompany eliminations

The work sheet showing intercompany eliminations on a GPL basis is shown as Exhibit M.

Exhibit M

ABC Company
Consolidated Work Sheet
General Price-Level Basis
December 31, 1974

	Consolidated Total Prior to 1974 Intercompany Eliminations	*1974 Intercompany Eliminations Dr.*	*1974 Intercompany Eliminations Cr.*	*Consolidated Total*
Inventories	$ 97,828		$ 258 (2)	$ 97,570
Receivable from parent	600		600 (3)	—
Other current assets	75,323			75,323
Investments	16,802			16,802
Fixed assets	371,168	$ 13 (5)	266 (4)	370,915
Other assets	709			709
Goodwill	852			852
	$563,282			$562,171
Payable to subsidiary	$ 600	600 (3)		
Other current liabilities	63,100			$ 63,100
Long-term debt	49,644			49,644
Deferred taxes	49,680			49,680
Share capital	174,546			174,546
Retained earnings	219,570	266 (4) 258 (2)	13 (5)	219,059
Price-level gain	1,420			1,420
Minority interest	4,722			4,722
	$563,282			$562,171

Exhibit M (continued)

	Consolidated Total Prior to 1974 Intercompany Eliminations	*1974 Intercompany Eliminations*		*Consolidated Total*
		Dr.	*Cr.*	
Sales	$465,217	266 (4) 2,126 (1)		$462,825
Other income	(422)			(422)
	$464,795			$462,403
Cost of sales	$297,590	258 (2)	2,126 (1)	$295,722
Selling and administrative	107,661			107,661
Depreciation	27,970		13 (5)	27,957
Interest	4,500			4,500
	$437,721			$435,840
	$ 27,074			$ 26,563
Income taxes	26,339			26,339
	$ 735			$ 224
Equity interest	313			313
Price-level gain	12,566			12,566
	$ 13,614			$ 13,103
Provisions	1,285			1,285
	$ 12,329			$ 11,818
Minority interest	32			32
Net income	$ 12,297			$ 11,786
Retained earnings	224,511			224,511
	$236,808			$236,297
Dividends	17,238			17,238
Retained earnings	$219,570	258 (2) 266 (4)	13 (5)	$219,059

Intercompany eliminations

(1) Elimination of intercompany sale of goods of $2,000 historical cost dollars. Sales are updated to December 1974 dollars by applying the average conversion factor for the year of 1.063. The amount to be eliminated is $2,000 × 1.063, i.e. $2,126.

(2) The $1,000 of the inventories included in ABC Company is included in the finished goods category of inventories. In restating the cost of finished goods of ABC Company the cost was updated by the conversion factor of 1.034 to restate into dollars of December 1974 value. The amounts in the

journal entries eliminating this transaction from the historical statements are restated by applying the same conversion factor. The profit elimination in the historical statements was $250; the profit eliminated in the GPL statement is therefore $250 × 1.034, i.e. $258.

(3) The elimination of the intercompany account payable and receivable.

(4) The profit on the sale of assets of its own manufacture by ABC Company to LMN Company Ltd., and the depreciation on the profit element eliminated in the historical cost statements are restated to the GPL basis by applying the same conversion factor used to update sales of ABC Company to dollars of December 1974 purchasing power value, i.e. 1.063. The profit eliminated in the historical cost statements was $250; in the price-level statements it is therefore $250 × 1.063, i.e. $266.

(5) The adjustment of depreciation provision as a result of (4) above, i.e. 5% on $266, or $13.

The net amount of fixed assets on a GPL basis is arrived at as follows:

	Restated cost	*Accumulated depreciation*	*Net*
Land	$ 11,237	—	$ 11,237
Other fixed assets			
Parent	$543,434	$197,751	
Subsidiary	22,232	7,984	
	$565,666	$205,735	
Intercompany elimination	266	13	
	$565,400	$205,722	359,678
			$370,915

The consolidated financial statements at December 31, 1974, on both the historical cost and the price-level basis are shown as Exhibits N and O.

Exhibit N

ABC Company
Consolidated Balance Sheet
December 31, 1974

	Historical	*Price-level*
ASSETS		
Current assets:		
Cash	$ 8,532	$ 8,532
Marketable securities	2,250	2,250
Accounts receivable	63,630	63,630
Inventories	97,550	97,570
Prepaid expenses	870	911
	$172,832	$172,893
Investments in associated companies	13,110	16,802
Fixed assets:		
Buildings, machinery and equipment	375,860	565,400
Less: Accumulated depreciation	(127,019)	(205,722)
Land	6,560	11,237
Other assets:		
Unamortized issue expense of long-term debt	413	709
Goodwill	2,247	852
	$444,003	$562,171
LIABILITIES AND SHAREHOLDERS' EQUITY		
Current liabilities:		
Bank loan	$ 5,160	$ 5,160
Accounts payable	51,810	51,810
Income taxes	5,760	5,760
Current portion of long-term debt	370	370
	$ 63,100	$ 63,100
Long-term debt	52,180	49,644
Deferred income taxes	49,680	49,680
Minority interest	3,441	4,722
Shareholders' equity:		
Share capital	80,450	174,546
Price-level gain on preferred shares		1,420
Retained earnings	189,752	219,059
Excess of appraised value of assets over cost	5,400	—
	$444,003	$562,171

Exhibit O

ABC Company
Consolidated Statement of Income and Retained Earnings

For the year ended December 31, 1974

	Historical	*Price-level*
Revenues:		
Sales	$435,395	$462,825
Investment income	140	149
Gain on sale of fixed assets	650	(571)
	$436,185	$462,403
Expenses:		
Cost of sales	263,223	295,722
Selling and administrative	101,190	107,661
Depreciation	18,707	27,957
Interest on long-term debt	4,221	4,500
	$387,341	$435,840
	$ 48,844	$ 26,563
Income taxes:		
Current	18,348	19,504
Deferred	6,430	6,835
	$ 24,778	$ 26,339
	$ 24,066	$ 224
Provision to reduce investments to market value	110	
	$ 23,956	$ 224
Equity in earnings of associated company	550	313
	$ 24,506	$ 537
Price-level adjustments:		
General price-level gain		8,431
Foreign currency debt		4,135
Reduction of investments to market value		(1,285)
		$ 11,281
	$ 24,506	$ 11,818
Minority interest	248	32
Net income	$ 24,258	$ 11,786
Retained earnings, beginning of year	181,607	224,511
	$205,865	$236,297
Dividends	16,113	17,238
Retained earnings, end of year	$189,752	$219,059

9

Consolidation—Fair Value Basis

When consolidated financial statements are prepared using the fair values assigned to the assets and liabilities of the subsidiary, the necessity of preparing separate GPL statements of the subsidiary depends upon whether or not the subsidiary is wholly-owned.

Where a subsidiary is wholly-owned and fair values were assigned to all assets and liabilities at the date of acquisition for purposes of consolidation, these amounts represent original cost to the parent company. These assets and liabilities can be merged with the assets and liabilities of the parent company and updated in similar fashion. Separate GPL statements of the subsidiary are not required.

Where a subsidiary is partly-owned, separate GPL statements of the subsidiary are required as the minority interest is calculated by reference to the separate price-level statements of the subsidiary.

Wholly-owned subsidiary

The December 1971 historical balance sheet of LMN Company Ltd. was illustrated on page 106. For purposes of the present illustration, assume the fair values shown below were assigned to the assets and liabilities at that date by ABC Company.

	Historical	*Fair values*
Cash	$ 55	$ 55
Receivables	1,105	1,090
Inventories	1,490	1,550
Fixed assets	9,338	12,000
	$11,988	$14,695
Current liabilities	1,650	1,650
Net assets acquired	$10,338	$13,045
Share capital	$ 8,000	
Retained earnings	2,338	
	$10,338	

If the cost of the acquisition had been $15,000 for all the shares of LMN Company Ltd., goodwill resulting from the acquisition would have been calculated in the following manner:

	Historical Book values	*Fair values*
Purchase price	$15,000	$15,000
Net assets acquired	10,338	13,045
	$ 4,662	$ 1,955

The consolidated balance sheet at date of acquisition on the historical cost basis would be prepared in the conventional manner using fair values of net assets acquired, and would show goodwill on acquisition of $1,955.

The GPL consolidated balance sheet at the date of acquisition would include the restated assets and liabilities of the parent company and the fair values of the assets and liabilities of the subsidiary at that date. Because the acquisition was made in December 1971 the fair values are already expressed in purchasing power at that date and no price-level restatement is necessary. If the acquisition had been made in an earlier month in 1971, the fair values would have had to be restated at December 31, 1971.

The goodwill arising on acquisition is the same amount in both the historical cost and price-level statements where fair values are assigned to the net assets acquired in the business combination. The purchase price is expressed in acquisition date dollars, the net assets being acquired are fair valued at the date of acquisition, and so are also expressed in acquisition date dollars.

GPL consolidated balance sheets at future year ends can be prepared by treating the assets and liabilities of any wholly-owned subsidiary as if they were the assets and liabilities of the parent company. When a subsidiary is wholly-owned, price-level adjustments are applied to the consolidated financial statements in the same manner as they are applied to the corporate financial statements of the parent company.

Partly-owned subsidiary

With the same illustration of ABC Company acquiring LMN Company Ltd. in December 1971, the statements of the subsidiary at date of acquisition are as summarized below.

	Historical		*Subsidiary's*
	Book values	*Fair values*	*Price-level 1971 $*
Cash	$ 55	$ 55	$ 55
Receivables	1,105	1,090	1,105
Inventories	1,490	1,550	1,512
Fixed assets	9,338	12,000	11,463
	$11,988	$14,695	$14,135
Current liabilities	1,650	1,650	1,650
	$10,338	$13,045	$12,485
Share capital	$ 8,000		$10,224
Retained earnings	2,338		2,261
	$10,338		$12,485

Calculation of goodwill on acquisition

If it is assumed ABC Company purchased 75% of the shares of LMN Company Ltd. at a cost of $10,000, goodwill resulting from the acquisition would have been as shown below. As already explained on page 136, goodwill is the same amount on both the historical and price-level bases when fair values are assigned to net assets at the date of acquisition because the fair values are already stated in terms of purchasing power at that date.

	Historical Fair values	*Parent's Price-level 1971 $*
Purchase price	$10,000	$10,000
Net assets acquired (75% of total net assets at fair values of $13,045)	9,784	9,784
	$ 216	$ 216

If it is assumed goodwill on acquisition is being retained on the consolidated balance sheet at original cost and not amortized, the entries in the consolidated and price-level statements are as follows:

	Historical Fair value basis	*Consolidated Price-level*
Goodwill, at cost		
December 1971 Balance sheet	$216	$216
December 1972 Balance sheet	$216	
Updated to 1972 dollars, 150/138, or 1.087		$235
December 1973 Balance sheet	$216	
Updated to 1973 dollars, 162/150, or 1.080		$254
December 1974 Balance sheet	$216	
Updated to 1974 dollars, 185/162, or 1.142		$289*

*See page 149.

Calculation of minority interest on acquisition

When fair values of the subsidiary's assets and liabilities are assigned only to the extent of the parent's interest, the minority interest is computed by reference to the subsidiary's own historical cost and GPL statements. Therefore the minority interest is the same whether the subsidiary is consolidated using book values or fair values. The minority interest is calculated as 25% of the carrying values on the subsidiary's own balance sheet.

	Historical consolidation		*Price-level*
	Book value	*Fair value*	*1971 $*
Total assets of subsidiary	$10,338	$13,045	$12,485
Minority interest, 25% of net assets on subsidiary's balance sheet	$ 2,585	$ 2,585	$ 3,121

The calculation of the minority interest at December 31, 1974 was illustrated on page 118; at that date the amounts were as follows.

	Historical	*Price-level 1974 $*
Minority interest	$3,441	$4,722

When fair values of the subsidiary's assets and liabilities are assigned to both the majority and minority interests, the calculation of the minority interest on acquisition is as illustrated on page 155.

Consolidating adjustments—historical cost basis

The work sheet for the consolidating adjustments at the date of acquisition and for 1972 to 1974 are set out as Exhibit P.

Exhibit P

ABC Company
Consolidated Work Sheet
Historical Cost Basis
December 31, 1974

	Parent	*Subsidiary*	*Consolidating Entries Dr.*	*Consolidating Entries Cr.*	*Consolidated Total Prior to 1974 Intercompany Eliminations*
Inventories	$ 96,050	$ 1,750			$ 97,800
Receivable from parent		600			600
Other current assets	70,290	4,992			75,282
Investments	23,110			$10,000 (1)	13,110
Fixed assets	246,486	9,152	$ 139 (8)		
			9,000 (8)	7,003 (8)	257,774
Other assets	413				413
Goodwill			216 (3)		216
	$436,349	$16,494			$445,195
Payable to subsidiary	$ 600				$ 600
Other current liabilities	60,370	$ 2,730			63,100
Long-term debt	52,180				52,180
Deferred taxes	49,680				49,680
Share capital	80,450	8,000	8,000 (2)		80,450
Retained earnings	187,669	5,764		139 (8)	
			3,194 (5)		
			34 (7)		190,344
Appraisal credit	5,400				5,400
Minority interest				3,441 (4)	3,441
	$436,349	$16,494			$445,195

Exhibit P (continued)

	Parent	*Subsidiary*	*Consolidating Entries* *Dr.*	*Consolidating Entries* *Cr.*	*Consolidated Total Prior to 1974 Intercompany Eliminations*
Sales	$427,745	$ 9,900			$437,645
Other income	790				790
	$428,535	$ 9,900			$438,435
Cost of sales	260,510	4,463			$264,973
Selling and administrative	98,340	2,850			101,190
Depreciation	18,108	612		47 (8)	18,673
Interest	4,221				4,221
	$381,179	$ 7,925			$389,057
	$ 47,356	$ 1,975			$ 49,378
Income taxes	23,798	980			24,778
	$ 23,558	$ 995			$ 24,600
Provisions	(110)				(110)
Equity interest	550				550
	$ 23,998	$ 995			$ 25,040
Minority interest			248 (6)		248
Net income	$ 23,998	$ 995			$ 24,792
Retained earnings	179,784	4,769	34 (7)	139 (8)	
			3,194 (5)	248 (6)	
			47 (8)		181,665
	$203,782	$ 5,764			$206,457
Dividends	16,113				16,113
Retained earnings	$187,669	$ 5,764			$190,344

Consolidating entries

(1) The elimination of the investment in the subsidiary carried in the parent's books at a cost of $10,000.

(2) The elimination of the subsidiary's share capital in the amount of $8,000.

(3) The setting up of goodwill on acquisition of $216 which is carried in the consolidated balance sheet at cost.

(4) The setting up of minority interest at its original amount at acquisition date plus the share of earnings to date, which amount is $3,441, being equivalent to 25% of the net assets of $13,764 of the subsidiary at December 1974.

(5) The removal from retained earnings of pre-acquisition profit and minority interest in subsequent earnings.

Retained earnings of subsidiary at date of acquisition		$2,338
Minority interest in earnings		
	1972 – $313	
	1973 – $295	
	1974 – $248	856
		$3,194

(6) The setting up of minority interest in 1974 earnings in the amount of $248.

The remaining adjustments arise because fair values assigned to the subsidiary's assets and liabilities must be substituted for the carrying values in the subsidiary's own amounts.

(7) The adjustment to the receivables and inventories at the date of acquisition affected the income statement for 1972 in the following manner:

(a) Profit was increased by $15 in respect of receivables which were adjusted to $1,090 from $1,105.

(b) Profit was reduced by $60 in respect of inventories which were adjusted to $1,550 from $1,490.

The profit reduction for 1972 was $45; as only 75% of the fair values of assets is being incorporated in the accounts, 75% of $45, i.e. $34, must be adjusted against opening retained earnings.

(8) The fixed assets were assigned fair values of $12,000 represented by

Assets being depreciated at 2½%	$ 5,000
Assets being depreciated at 5%	7,000
	$12,000

As fair values are assigned to only the 75% of the assets purchased by the parent company, 75% of the net assets on the subsidiary's books at date of acquisition (i.e. 75% of $9,338 = $7,003) must be replaced by 75% of the fair values at date of acquisition (i.e. 75% of $12,000 = $9,000).

An adjustment must also be made to substitute depreciation on the subsidiary's assets at fair values for depreciation based on book values. The adjustment is calculated in the following manner:

Depreciation charged by subsidiary on book values of fixed assets on hand at date of acquisition. (See page 112.)		$537
Depreciation calculated by reference to fair values ascribed to fixed assets at date of acquisition		
2½% on $5,000	$125	
5% on $7,000	350	475
		$ 62
Reduction in depreciation to reflect substitution of fair values for book values from 1972 to 1974		$186
75% thereof		$139

A similar adjustment in respect of 1974 is made in the 1974 historical income statement and is calculated as follows.

1974 depreciation based on	
restated book values	$537
fair values	475
	$ 62
Adjustment, being 75% thereof	$ 47

The foregoing adjustments relate only to the fixed assets to which fair values were assigned at the acquisition date and therefore do not include depreciation provided in 1974 on additions made in that year.

Intercompany eliminations

Intercompany transactions which take place after the date of acquisition are unaffected by the consolidation being based on book values or on fair values, except for any transfer of fixed assets held at date of acquisition from the subsidiary to the parent company.

The elimination on a historical basis of intercompany transactions which took place in 1974 would be identical to those illustrated on page 124. The work sheet showing intercompany eliminations for the year 1974 is shown as Exhibit Q.

Exhibit Q

ABC Company
Consolidated Work Sheet
Historical Cost Basis
December 31, 1974

	Consolidated Total Prior to 1974 Intercompany Eliminations	*1974 Intercompany Eliminations Dr.*	*1974 Intercompany Eliminations Cr.*	*Consolidated Total*
Inventories	$ 97,800		$ 250 (2)	$ 97,550
Receivable from parent	600		600 (3)	
Other current assets	75,282			75,282
Investments	13,110			13,110
Fixed assets	257,774	$ 13 (5)	250 (4)	257,537
Other assets	413			413
Goodwill	216			216
	$445,195			$444,108
Payable to subsidiary	$ 600	600 (3)		
Other current liabilities	63,100			$ 63,100
Long-term debt	52,180			52,180
Deferred taxes	49,680			49,680
Share capital	80,450			80,450
Retained earnings	190,344	250 (4)	13 (5)	
		250 (2)		189,857
Appraisal credit	5,400			5,400
Minority interest	3,441			3,441
	$445,195			$444,108

Exhibit Q (continued)

	Consolidated Total Prior to 1974 Intercompany Eliminations	*1974 Intercompany Eliminations*		*Consolidated Total*
		Dr.	*Cr.*	
Sales	$437,645	2,000 (1) 250 (4)		$435,395
Other income	790			790
	$438,435			$436,185
Cost of sales	$264,973	250 (2)	2,000 (1)	$263,223
Selling and administrative	101,190			101,190
Depreciation	18,673		13 (5)	18,660
Interest	4,221			4,221
	$389,057			$387,294
	$ 49,378			$ 48,891
Income taxes	24,778			24,778
	$ 24,600			$ 24,113
Provisions	(110)			(110)
Equity interest	550			550
	$ 25,040			$ 24,553
Minority interest	248			248
Net income	$ 24,792			$ 24,305
Retained earnings	181,665			181,665
	$206,457			$205,970
Dividends	16,113			16,113
Retained earnings	$190,344	250 (2) 250 (4)	13 (5)	$189,857

Consolidating adjustments—price-level basis

The work sheet for the consolidating adjustments at date of acquisition and for 1972 to 1974 on a GPL basis is shown as Exhibit R.

Exhibit R

ABC Company
Consolidated Work Sheet
General Price-Level Basis
December 31, 1974

	Parent	Subsidiary	Consolidating Entries Dr.	Consolidating Entries Cr.	Consolidated Total Prior to 1974 Intercompany Eliminations
Inventories	$ 96,050	$ 1,778			$ 97,828
Receivable from parent		600			600
Other current assets	70,331	4,992			75,323
Investments	30,209	—		$13,407 (1)	16,802
Fixed assets	356,920	14,248	$ 552 (8)	11,526 (8)	
			12,066 (8)		372,260
Other assets	709				709
Goodwill			289 (3)		289
	$554,219	$21,618			$563,811
Payable to subsidiary	$ 600	$ —			$ 600
Other current liabilities	60,370	2,730			63,100
Long-term debt	49,644				49,644
Deferred taxes	49,680				49,680
Share capital	174,546	13,707	13,707 (2)		174,546
Retained earnings	217,959	5,181	3,570 (5)	552 (8)	
			23 (7)		220,099
Price-level gain	1,420				1,420
Minority interest				4,722 (4)	4,722
	$554,219	$21,618			$563,811

Exhibit R (continued)

	Parent	Subsidiary	Consolidating entries Dr.	Consolidating entries Cr.	Consolidated Total Prior to 1974 Intercompany Eliminations
Sales	$454,693	$10,524			$465,217
Other income	(422)				(422)
	$454,271	$10,524			$464,795
Cost of sales	292,622	4,968			$297,590
Selling and administrative	104,631	3,030			107,661
Depreciation	27,009	961		184 (8)	27,786
Interest	4,500				4,500
	$428,762	$ 8,959			$437,537
	$ 25,509	$ 1,565			$ 27,258
Income taxes	25,297	1,042			26,339
	$ 212	$ 523			$ 919
Equity interest	313				313
Price-level gain (loss)	12,962	(396)			12,566
	$ 13,487	$ 127			$ 13,798
Provisions	1,285				1,285
	$ 12,202	$ 127			$ 12,513
Minority interest			32 (6)		32
Net income	$ 12,202	$ 127			$ 12,481
Retained earnings	222,995	5,054	3,570 (5)	32 (6)	
			23 (7)	552 (8)	
			184 (8)		224,856
	$235,197	$ 5,181			$237,337
Dividends	17,238				17,238
Retained earnings	$217,959	$ 5,181			$220,099

Consolidating entries

(1) The elimination of the investment in the subsidiary, carried in the parent's price-level statements at its restated cost of $13,407 in 1974 dollars.

(2) The elimination of the subsidiary's share capital in its restated amount of $13,707 in 1974 dollars.

(3) The setting up of goodwill on acquisition of $216 in 1971 dollars restated to $289 in 1974 dollars.

(4) The setting up of minority interest at its original restated amount at the acquisition date, plus the share of earnings to date, all expressed in 1974 dollars, which amount is $4,722 being equivalent to 25% of the net assets of $18,888 in the GPL balance sheet of the subsidiary at December 31, 1974.

(5) The removal from retained earnings of pre-acquisition profit and minority interest in subsequent earnings

Retained earnings of subsidiary at date of acquisition in 1971 dollars	$2,261	
equivalent in 1972 dollars at 1.087	$2,458	
equivalent in 1973 dollars at 1.080	$2,655	
equivalent in 1974 dollars at 1.142		$3,032
Minority interest in earnings, expressed in 1974 dollars		
1972 – $260 × 1.080 × 1.142	$ 321	
1973 – $162 × 1.142	185	
1974 – $32	32	538
		$3,570

(6) The setting up of minority interest in 1974 earnings in the restated amount of $32.

The remaining adjustments arise because fair values assigned to the subsidiary's assets and liabilities must be substituted for the restated values in the subsidiary's own GPL statements.

(7) Receivables were assigned a fair value of $1,090, which replaced the amount in the GPL balance sheet of that date of $1,105, i.e. an increase in profit of $15 expressed in 1971 dollars which is equivalent to $19 in 1974 dollars.

Inventories were assigned a fair value of $1,550, which replaced the amount in the GPL balance sheet of that date of $1,512, i.e. a decrease in profit of $38 expressed in 1971 dollars which is equivalent to $50 in 1974 dollars.

As only 75% of the fair values is being substituted the amount to be adjusted is 75% of ($50 — 19), i.e. $23.

(8) The fixed assets were fair valued at an amount of $12,000

Assets depreciated on the straight-line basis	
at 2½ %	$ 5,000
at 5%	7,000
	$12,000

The asset amounts are updated each year as if they had been acquired at December 1971.

		1972	*1973*	*1974*
Conversion factors		1.087	1.080	1.142
Original cost	$ 5,000	$ 5,435	$ 5,870	$ 6,703
	7,000	7,609	8,218	9,385
	$12,000	$13,044	$14,088	$16,088

As fair values are assigned to only 75% of the assets purchased by the parent company, 75% of the net fixed assets on the subsidiary's GPL statements at date of acquisition (i.e. 75% of $11,463 = $8,597 or $11,526 expressed in 1974 dollars) is replaced by 75% of the fair values of fixed assets at date of acquisition (i.e. 75% of $16,088 = $12,066 expressed in 1974 dollars).

The depreciation charge is also adjusted to replace the amount charged on the subsidiary's assets at their restated book values by the amount calculated by reference to their restated fair values. The adjustment in respect of 1972 to 1974 is calculated in 1974 dollars in the following manner.

Depreciation charged by subsidiary on restated book values of fixed assets on hand at date of acquisition (see page 110)		
1972 – $714 × 1.080 × 1.142	$ 881	
1973 – $772 × 1.142	881	
1974 – $881	881	
	$2,643	
75% thereof		$1,983
Depreciation calculated by reference to fair values ascribed to fixed assets at date of acquisition, i.e. $475 in 1971 dollars (see page 142)		

Annual charge updated to 1974 dollars $475 × 1.087 × 1.080 × 1.142	$ 636	
Aggregate charge, 1972 to 1974, in 1974 dollars	$1,908	
75% thereof		1,431
Reduction in depreciation charge from 1972 to 1974 to reflect substitution of fair values for book values – majority shareholders' proportion		$ 552

A similar adjustment in respect of 1974 is made in the 1974 GPL income statement and is calculated as follows:

1974 depreciation –	
restated book values	$ 881
fair values	636
	$ 245
Adjustment, being 75% thereof	$ 184

Differences in GPL consolidating adjustments

It should be noted that small differences attributable to rounding may arise in the consolidation of GPL statements. Thus, in GPL statements of the parent, the investment in the subsidiary and goodwill accounts will be rolled forward year by year from the date of acquisition of the subsidiary. Each year these figures may be rounded after being restated by application of the appropriate conversion factor. At the same time, the GPL statements of the subsidiary will be rolled forward and the assets and liabilities may similarly be rounded on restatement. It follows that the rounding in the GPL statements of the subsidiary may not exactly correspond with the rounding in the parent company's investment and goodwill accounts, and minor differences may emerge when the consolidation is prepared. Any such difference must be recognized in the consolidating adjustments; in Exhibit R the difference amounts to $1 and has been adjusted through goodwill.

Intercompany eliminations

Intercompany transactions which take place after the date of acquisition are unaffected by the consolidation being based on book values or on fair values, except for any transfer of fixed assets held at date of acquisition from the subsidiary to the parent company.

The elimination of intercompany transactions which took place in 1974 on a GPL basis would be identical to those illustrated on page 130 to which these eliminations are cross-referenced. The work sheet showing intercompany eliminations for the year 1974 is shown as Exhibit S.

Exhibit S

ABC Company
Consolidated Work Sheet
General Price-Level Basis
December 31, 1974

	Consolidated Total Prior to 1974 Intercompany Eliminations	*1974 Intercompany Eliminations*		*Consolidated Total*
		Dr.	*Cr.*	
Inventories	$ 97,828		$ 258 (2)	$ 97,570
Receivable from parent	600		600 (3)	
Other current assets	75,323			75,323
Investments	16,802			16,802
Fixed assets	372,260	$ 13 (5)	266 (4)	372,007
Other assets	709			709
Goodwill	289			289
	$563,811			$562,700
Payable to subsidiary	$ 600	600 (3)		
Other current liabilities	63,100			$ 63,100
Long-term debt	49,644			49,644
Deferred taxes	49,680			49,680
Share capital	174,546			174,546
Retained earnings	220,099	258 (2)		
		266 (4)	13 (5)	219,588
Price-level gain	1,420			1,420
Minority interest	4,722			4,722
	$563,811			$562,700

Exhibit S (continued)

	Consolidated Total Prior to 1974 Intercompany Eliminations	*1974 Intercompany Eliminations Dr.*	*1974 Intercompany Eliminations Cr.*	*Consolidated Total*
Sales	$465,217			
		266 (4)		
		2,126 (1)		$462,825
Other income	(422)			(422)
	$464,795			$462,403
Cost of sales	$297,590	258 (2)	2,126 (1)	$295,722
Selling and administrative	107,661			107,661
Depreciation	27,786		13 (5)	27,773
Interest	4,500			4,500
	$437,537			$435,656
	$ 27,258			$ 26,747
Income taxes	26,339			26,339
	$ 919			$ 408
Equity interest	313			313
Price-level gain (loss)	12,566			12,566
	$ 13,798			$ 13,287
Provisions	1,285			1,285
	$ 12,513			$ 12,002
Minority interest	32			32
Net income	$ 12,481			$ 11,970
Retained earnings	224,856			224,856
	$237,337			$236,826
Dividends	17,238			17,238
		266 (4)	13 (5)	
Retained earnings	$220,099	258 (2)		$219,588

The consolidated financial statements at December 31, 1974 on the historical and GPL bases are shown as Exhibits T and U. Fixed asset cost and accumulated depreciation on both bases are analyzed as follows:

Historical basis	*Cost*	*Accumulated depreciation*	*Net*
Land	$ 6,560		$ 6,560
Other fixed assets			
Parent	$362,110	$122,184	
Subsidiary			
Parent's share (75% of fair values)			
75% of $12,000	9,000		
75% of $ 1,425		1,069	
Minority's share (25% of book values)			
25% of $12,500	3,125		
25% of $ 4,773		1,193	
Additions in 1974	1,500	75	
	$375,735	$124,521	
Intercompany elimination	250	13	
	$375,485	$124,508	250,977
			$257,537

GPL basis	*Restated cost*	*Accumulated depreciation*	*Net*
Land	$ 11,237		$ 11,237
Other fixed assets			
Parent	$543,434	$197,751	
Subsidiary			
Parent's share (75% of restated fair values)			
75% of $16,088	12,066		
75% of $ 1,908		1,431	
Minority's share (25% of restated book values)			
25% of $20,628	5,157		
25% of $ 7,904		1,976	
Additions in 1974	1,604	80	
	$562,261	$201,238	
Intercompany elimination	266	13	
	$561,995	$201,225	360,770
			$372,007

Exhibit T

ABC Company
Consolidated Balance Sheet
December 31, 1974

	Historical	*Price-level*
ASSETS		
Current assets:		
Cash	$ 8,532	$ 8,532
Marketable securities	2,250	2,250
Accounts receivable	63,630	63,630
Inventories	97,550	97,570
Prepaid expenses	870	911
	$172,832	$172,893
Investment in associated companies	13,110	16,802
Fixed assets:		
Buildings, machinery and equipment	375,485	561,995
Less: Accumulated depreciation	(124,508)	(201,225)
Land	6,560	11,237
Other assets:		
Unamortized issue expense of long-term debt	413	709
Goodwill	216	289
	$444,108	$562,700
LIABILITIES AND SHAREHOLDERS' EQUITY		
Current liabilities:		
Bank loan	$ 5,160	$ 5,160
Accounts payable	51,810	51,810
Income taxes	5,760	5,760
Current portion of long-term debt	370	370
	$ 63,100	$ 63,100
Long-term debt	52,180	49,644
Deferred income taxes	49,680	49,680
Minority interest	3,441	4,722
Shareholders' equity:		
Share capital	80,450	174,546
Price-level gain on preferred shares		1,420
Retained earnings	189,857	219,588
Excess of appraised value of assets over cost	5,400	—
	$444,108	$562,700

Exhibit U

ABC Company
Consolidated Statement of Income and Retained Earnings
For the year ended December 31, 1974

	Historical	*Price-level*
Revenues:		
Sales	$435,395	$462,825
Investment income	140	149
Gain on sale of fixed assets	650	(571)
	$436,185	$462,403
Expenses:		
Cost of sales	$263,223	$295,722
Selling and administrative	101,190	107,661
Depreciation	18,660	27,773
Interest on long-term debt	4,221	4,500
	$387,294	$435,656
	$ 48,891	$ 26,747
Income taxes:		
Current	18,348	19,504
Deferred	6,430	6,835
	$ 24,778	$ 26,339
	$ 24,113	$ 408
Provision to reduce investments to market value	110	—
	$ 24,003	$ 408
Equity in earnings of associated company	550	313
	$ 24,553	$ 721
Price-level adjustments:		
General price-level gain		8,431
Foreign currency debt		4,135
Reduction of investments to market value		(1,285)
		$ 11,281
	$ 24,553	$ 12,002
Minority interest	248	32
Net income	$ 24,305	$ 11,970
Retained earnings, beginning of year	181,665	224,856
	$205,970	$236,826
Dividends	16,113	17,238
Retained earnings, end of year	$189,857	$219,588

Calculation of minority interest when fair values assigned to parent and minority interests

When fair values of the subsidiary's assets and liabilities are assigned to both the majority and minority interests, the minority interest at date of acquisition is computed at its proportionate share of these fair values.

	Historical consolidation *Fair values*	*Price-level* *1971 $*
Total net assets of subsidiary	$13,045	$13,045
Minority interest, 25%	$ 3,261	$ 3,261

The calculation of minority interest for years subsequent to the acquisition is shown below and is based on the separate GPL statements of the subsidiary. These are adjusted, in the same way as the historical statements, to replace the restated cost of assets with the fair values assigned to those assets at the acquisition; the related depreciation is similarly restated.

		Historical		*Price-level*
Minority interest at acquisition		$3,261		$3,261
1972 Restated to 1972 dollars at 1.087				$3,545
Earnings of subsidiary in own statements (see page 109)	$1,251		$1,041	
Add depreciation (see pages 110 and 112)	537		714	
	$1,788		$1,755	
Less depreciation on fair values (see page 142)	475		516(2)	
	$1,313		$1,239	
Add increase in profit arising from adjustment of 1971 receivables to fair values	15		16	
	$1,328		$1,255	
Less decrease in profit arising from adjustment of 1971 inventories to fair values	60		41(1)	
	$1,268		$1,214	
25% thereof		$ 317		303
		$3,578		$3,848
1973 Restated to 1973 dollars at 1.080				$4,156
Earnings of subsidiary in own statements	$1,180		$ 648	
Add depreciation	537		772	
	$1,717		$1,420	
Less depreciation on fair values	475		557(2)	
	$1,242		$ 863	
25% thereof		311		216
		$3,889		$4,372

	Historical		*Price-level*	
1974 Restated to 1974 dollars at 1.142				$4,993
Earnings of subsidiary in own statements	$ 995		$ 127	
Add depreciation	537		881	
	$1,532		$1,008	
Less depreciation on fair values	475		636(2)	
	$1,057		$ 372	
25% thereof		264		93
		$4,153		$5,086

(1) The GPL restatement of the decrease in 1972 profit arising from the adjustment of 1971 inventories to fair values is arrived at in the following way:

Fair values assigned to inventories	$1,550
Inventories in GPL statement	1,512
In 1971 dollars	$ 38
Restated to 1972 dollars, at 1.087	$ 41

(2) Depreciation based on fair values

On fair values at date of acquisition in 1971 dollars	$ 475
Restated to 1972 dollars, at 1.087	$ 516
Restated to 1973 dollars, at 1.080	$ 557
Restated to 1974 dollars, at 1.142	$ 636

10

Consolidation of a Foreign Subsidiary

The problems of translating the historical financial statements of foreign subsidiaries from their foreign currency amounts into statements expressed in the domestic currency of the parent company have concerned accountants for many years. It is not the intention of this book to reiterate those problems which are still under study.

In GPL accounting, the problem arising on consolidation of a foreign subsidiary can be summed up in a question.

Should the foreign subsidiary's historical statements be translated into the domestic currency of the parent company, and then restated by reference to the inflation rate of the parent company's country? (the "translate-restate" method).

or

Should the foreign subsidiary's historical statements be restated into GPL statements by reference to the rate of inflation in the foreign country, and then translated into the domestic currency of the parent? (the "restate-translate" method).

The "translate-restate" method

Under this method, the financial statements of the foreign subsidiary, expressed in foreign currency, are translated into the parent company's domestic currency. In Canada and the United States the methods of translation most frequently used have been the current/non-current and monetary/non-monetary; in the United States the temporal method is also used, while in the United Kingdom translation is commonly made at the current rate of exchange. The translated statements can then be considered equivalent to the statements of a domestic subsidiary and can be restated on a price-level basis, using the same indices as the parent company.

Translation in historical statements is an accounting process by which amounts measured in a foreign currency are translated into the currency with which the readers of domestic financial statements are familiar. In a historical cost context translation merely converts amounts in a foreign currency to amounts in the currency of the parent company. In a price-level context there is an added dimension; not only is the currency to be translated into one with which the reader is familiar, but the result will also recognize a degree of inflation applicable to that currency. Thus the theory of the translate-restate method is that it applies to the translated foreign currency amounts the inflation rate applicable to the parent company's currency and not to the foreign currency. As a result GPL consolidated statements are presented in terms of a single unit of measurement which reflects the general purchasing power of the parent company's currency.

The method of applying the normal realization test to the assets of a foreign subsidiary involves two stages when the translate-restate method is used. In the first stage, the realizable value (or in the case of fixed assets, the recoverable value to the business) is determined in the foreign currency and then translated at the year-end rate of exchange into the currency of the parent company. In the second stage, the translated amount is compared with the restated cost of the asset for evidence of any impairment of value.

The "restate-translate" method

Under this approach the financial statements of the foreign subsidiary, expressed in foreign currency, are restated on a GPL basis using indices which reflect the changes in the purchasing power of the foreign currency. These GPL statements are then translated into the domestic currency of the parent country using the year-end rate of exchange and consolidated with the GPL statements of the parent company.

This method recognizes that the subsidiary is operating in a foreign country and is subject to the economic climate of that country; therefore, the financial statements of the subsidiary should reflect the changes in the purchasing power of its currency. Furthermore, the rate of inflation in the country of the parent company is not relevant to the financial statements of a foreign subsidiary. These arguments hold considerable weight if GPL statements are presented as the primary financial statements of the subsidiary; this may be the case if the subsidiary operates in a country where the degree of inflation has become so great that financial statements prepared on the historical cost basis have lost their significance.

On the other hand, the restate-translate method uses conversion factors based on national indices that are not of interest or relevance to the parent company or its shareholders. If one accepts that the primary purpose of foreign investment is to produce a return which eventually will flow back to the parent company, the restate-translate method is inconsistent with this philosophy.

In considering the restate-translate method, the availability of appropriate indices in the foreign country is a matter of importance. In many countries appropriate indices are prepared, but in other countries indices may not be available or may not be available on a timely basis. This would in effect prevent the use of the restate-translate method.

Authoritative pronouncements on the treatment of foreign subsidiaries

In the United States, APB Statement No. 3 issued in 1969 advocated the translate-restate method.

> "Restatement of financial statements of foreign branches or subsidiaries of U.S. companies for inclusion in combined or consolidated financial statements stated in terms of U.S. dollars should be based on an index of the general level of prices in the United States. General price-level financial statements stated in terms of U.S. dollars use a unit of measure that represents the general purchasing power of the U.S. dollar at a specified date. An index of changes in the general purchasing power of the U.S. dollar should therefore be used to restate the financial statements of a company and its combined or consolidated foreign branches and subsidiaries. Financial statements of foreign branches or subsidiaries to be combined or consolidated with the financial statements of their United States parent company should first be translated into U.S. dollars using presently accepted methods and then restated for changes in the general purchasing power of the U.S. dollar."

This position has been maintained by the FASB in its exposure draft issued in 1974.

> "52. Financial statements of foreign branches, subsidiaries, and other investees that are expressed in units of a foreign currency shall first be translated into U.S. dollars and then be restated for changes in the general purchasing power of the U.S. dollar in accordance with the provisions of this Statement."
>
> "80. An objective of general purchasing power accounting is to express all amounts in a single unit of measure, namely, units

> of the general purchasing power of a single currency such as the U.S. dollar. Accordingly, the Board has required that financial statements of foreign branches, subsidiaries, and other investees first be translated into U.S. dollars and then restated for changes in the dollar's general purchasing power (see paragraph 52). The alternative, restatement for changes in the purchasing power of a foreign currency prior to translation, would result in an intermingling of units of the general purchasing power of the dollar and units of the general purchasing power of a foreign currency and would, therefore, be inconsistent with the objective stated above."

In the United Kingdom, however, provisional SSAP No. 7 does not recommend which method should be used.

> "The supplementary statement should contain a note outlining the method of conversion used including the treatment of accounts originally prepared in foreign currencies."

Practical aspects

In Chapter 11, the translate-restate and the restate-translate methods are illustrated and the application of both methods is demonstrated by reference to a British and a South American subsidiary of a Canadian company. It is readily apparent that different results are likely to be obtained according to which method is used; it may be expected that the different degrees of inflation in the United Kingdom and in South America will also have a bearing on the results obtained.

The latter is to some extent true, but probably less so than might be imagined. The fact of a higher rate of inflation in the South American country is largely reflected in the decrease in the value of the South American currency against the Canadian currency. There are of course other factors which influence movements in rates of exchange, but the effect of different rates of inflation can be expected to exert a major influence. It follows that if the difference in rates of inflation is compensated by a difference in the rates of exchange, the results of applying the translate-restate method will more closely approximate those of the restate-translate method. However, the results will never be identical because movement in the rate of exchange cannot completely equalize the effects of inflation, particularly in the space of one accounting period.

In practical terms, the translate-restate method has the advantages of:

- measuring the effect of changes in the purchasing power of the parent company's currency, which is the unit that has meaning and relevance to the shareholder for whom the consolidated statements are prepared, and
- permitting the updating of consolidated statements as a whole when the subsidiary is wholly owned, so avoiding the need to prepare a second consolidation of rolled-forward GPL statements for each subsidiary.

Nevertheless, the possible use of the restate-translate method should not be completely disregarded. As mentioned already, the method could be expected to be advantageous when a subsidiary operates in a country that has experienced acute inflation and as a result issues price-level adjusted statements as its primary financial statements. There is also perhaps a tendency for the restate-translate method to be followed by companies which use the current rate method for translation of historical cost transactions and financial statements.

So far as practical application of the restate-translate method is concerned, it is worth observing that the parent company's investment in the subsidiary, when restated to reflect changes in the purchasing power of the parent company's currency, will not equal the parent company's equity in the subsidiary's GPL statements after translation. The difference arises because the investment account of the parent company has been restated by reference to a national index while the underlying net assets have been restated by reference to a foreign index. This difference would be treated as a debit or credit in the consolidated GPL income statement.

11

Illustration of "Translate-Restate" and "Restate-Translate" Methods

To illustrate the procedures for applying the translate-restate and restate-translate methods, assume that the following are the statements of a foreign company at December 31, 1974.

		Foreign currency
Cash	FC	500
Receivables		2,500
Fixed assets (acquired December 1972)		8,000
	FC	11,000
Payables	FC	3,500
Share capital (issued December 1972)		6,000
Retained earnings		1,500
	FC	11,000

Assumptions

1. Rates of exchange
   December 1972 FC 2.50 = $1.00
   December 1974 FC 3.00 = $1.00
2. Indices in home country
   December 1972 150
   December 1974 185
3. Indices in foreign country
   December 1972 254
   December 1974 485

The following results would be obtained by applying the two methods.

	Translate-restate	*Restate-translate*
Cash	(1) $ 167	(1) $ 167
Receivables	(1) 833	(1) 833
Fixed assets	(2) 3,946	(5) 5,091
	$4,946	$6,091
Payables	(1) $1,167	(1) $1,167
Share capital	(3) 2,959	(6) 3,818
Retained earnings	(4) 820	(4) 1,106
	$4,946	$6,091

(1) Translated at closing rate of exchange; monetary item

(2) Translated at historical rate of exchange i.e. $3,200; non-monetary item updated at 185/150 or 1.233

(3) Translated at historical rate of exchange i.e. $2,400; non-monetary item updated at 185/150 or 1.233

(4) Balancing amount

(5) Non-monetary item updated at 485/254 or 1.909 i.e. FC 15,272 translated at closing rate of exchange, i.e. $5,091.

(6) Non-monetary item updated at 485/254 or 1.909 i.e. FC 11,454 translated at closing rate of exchange, i.e. $3,818.

This illustration shows that the results obtained under the two methods will vary; the amount of the variance will depend partly on the differences between the rates of inflation in the parent company's country and in the foreign country and partly on the fluctuations in the exchange rates of the currencies concerned.

The effects of the two methods can be illustrated by reference to:

(a) a subsidiary located in a foreign country where the inflation rate is fairly similar to that of the parent company's country, and

(b) a subsidiary located in a foreign country where the inflation rate is significantly different to that of the parent company's country.

Assume that ABC Company, a Canadian company, acquired:

1. UK Company Ltd., a company located in the United Kingdom
2. RST Company, a company located in South America.

Subsidiary located in the United Kingdom

The following are the historical statements of the United Kingdom subsidiary, expressed in pounds sterling.

	December 31	
Balance sheet	*1973*	*1974*
Cash	£ 1,000	
Receivables	1,500	£ 1,800
Inventories	3,300	3,800
Fixed assets	28,000	36,000
Less: Accumulated depreciation	(18,200)	(21,800)
	£15,600	£19,800
Bank loan		£ 1,100
Payables	£ 3,100	5,100
Share capital	8,000	8,000
Retained earnings	4,500	5,600
	£15,600	£19,800

Statement of income and retained earnings	*For the year ended December 31, 1974*
Sales	£16,300
Cost of sales	9,800
Depreciation	3,600
Selling and administrative expenses	800
	£14,200
	£ 2,100
Income taxes	1,000
Net income	£ 1,100
Retained earnings, beginning of year	4,500
Retained earnings, end of year	£ 5,600

Assumptions as to indices and exchange rates

	Canada	*United Kingdom*		
1966 average	112	60	£1.00 =	$3.00
1968 average	122	65		$2.60
1972 average	142	85		$2.50
1973 year-end	162	98		$2.30
1974 average	174	104		$2.32
1974 June	173	105		$2.32
1974 year-end	185	110		$2.30

The "translate-restate" method

Under this method the statements must first be translated into Canadian dollars and then restated on a GPL basis using the Canadian indices. The first statement to be translated (using the current/non-current method) and updated is the December 1973 balance sheet.

Exhibit V shows the 1973 sterling balance sheet, translated into Canadian dollars and expressed on a price-level basis in both 1973 and 1974 dollars.

Exhibit V

UK Company Ltd.
Balance Sheet
December 31, 1973

	Historical		*Price-level*	
	Sterling	*Dollars*	*1973 $*	*1974 $*
Cash	£ 1,000	$ 2,300	$ 2,300	$ 2,627
Receivables	1,500	3,450	3,450	3,940
Inventories	3,300	7,590	7,636	8,720
Fixed assets	28,000	79,100	108,725	124,164
Less: Accumulated depreciation	(18,200)	(52,660)	(74,279)	(84,827)
	£15,600	$39,780	$ 47,832	$ 54,624
Payables	£ 3,100	$ 7,130	$ 7,130	$ 8,142
Share capital	8,000	24,000	34,704	39,632
Retained earnings	4,500	8,650	5,998	6,850
	£15,600	$39,780	$ 47,832	$ 54,624

Translating the 1973 historical balance sheet

The balance sheet is translated from pounds sterling into Canadian dollars using the current/non-current method of translation.

(1) All current items, i.e. cash, receivables, inventory and payables, are translated at the closing rate of exchange at December 1973 of £1.00 = $2.30.

(2) The fixed assets must be analyzed into their year of acquisition and converted at rates prevailing on those dates. Depreciation is at a rate of 10% per annum calculated on the straight-line basis.

	Sterling			*Dollars*	
Year of acquisition	*Cost*	*Acc. dep.*	*Exchange rate*	*Cost*	*Acc. dep.*
1966	£17,000	£13,600	£1 = $3.00	$51,000	$40,800
1968	6,000	3,600	£1 = $2.60	15,600	9,360
1972	5,000	1,000	£1 = $2.50	12,500	2,500
	£28,000	£18,200		$79,100	$52,660

(3) The share capital was issued in 1966 and is translated at the exchange rate for that year of £1 Sterling = \$3.00.

(4) The retained earnings is a balancing figure.

Converting the 1973 translated balance sheet to a price-level basis

The translated balance sheet in historical Canadian dollars is updated to December 1973 dollars by the application of Canadian indices.

(1) The monetary items are cash, receivables and payables and require no restatement.

(2) The inventories were acquired during the last three months of 1973 when the average index was say 161. The inventory is therefore updated

$$\$7{,}590 \times 162/161, \text{ or } 1.006 = \$7{,}636$$

(3) The fixed assets are updated by reference to the indices applicable to their years of acquisition.

Year of acquisition	*Historical Cost*	*Historical Acc. dep.*	*Conversion factor*	*Price-level 1973 \$ Cost*	*Price-level 1973 \$ Acc. dep.*
1966	\$51,000	\$40,800	162/112, or 1.446	\$ 73,746	\$58,997
1968	15,600	9,360	162/122, or 1.328	20,717	12,430
1972	12,500	2,500	162/142, or 1.141	14,262	2,852
	\$79,100	\$52,660		\$108,725	\$74,279

(4) The share capital was issued in 1966 and is updated by using the index applicable to that year

$$\$24{,}000 \times 162/112, \text{ or } 1.446 = \$34{,}704$$

(5) The retained earnings is again a balancing item.

Rolling forward the 1973 price-level balance sheet to 1974 price-levels

The 1973 GPL balance sheet is rolled forward to its equivalent in dollars of December 1974 purchasing power by applying the conversion factor appropriate to the index at the end of 1974 divided by the index at the end of 1973, i.e. 185/162, or 1.142.

* * *

Exhibit W shows the 1974 sterling balance sheet, translated into Canadian dollars and expressed on a price-level basis in 1974 dollars.

Exhibit X shows the 1974 sterling statement of income and retained earnings, translated into Canadian dollars and expressed on a price-level basis in 1974 dollars.

Translating the 1974 historical balance sheet

As in 1973 the balance sheet is translated from pounds sterling to Canadian dollars by use of the current/non-current method of translation.

(1) All current items, i.e. bank loan, receivables, inventory, and payables are translated at the closing rate of exchange at December 1974 of £1.00 = $2.30 Canadian.

(2) The fixed asset and depreciation accounts are translated at historical rates and include the acquisitions made in June 1974 and the depreciation provision for 1974.

Year of acquisition	*Sterling*			*Dollars*		
		Depreciation			*Depreciation*	
	Cost	*to 1973*	*1974*	*Cost*	*to 1973*	*1974*
1966	£17,000	£13,600	£ 1,700	$51,000	$40,800	$ 5,100
1968	6,000	3,600	600	15,600	9,360	1,560
1972	5,000	1,000	500	12,500	2,500	1,250
	£28,000	£18,200	£ 2,800	$79,100	$52,660	$ 7,910
1974 June	8,000		800	18,560		1,856
	£36,000	£18,200	£ 3,600	$97,660	$52,660	$ 9,766
			18,200			52,660
			£21,800			$62,426

(3) The share capital is translated at the rate of exchange prevailing when it was issued in 1966 of £1.00 = $3.00.

(4) The retained earnings is a balancing figure.

Exhibit W

UK Company Ltd.
Balance Sheet
December 31, 1974

	Historical Basis		Price-level Basis
	Sterling	Dollars	1974 $
Receivables	£ 1,800	$ 4,140	$ 4,140
Inventories	3,800	8,740	8,880
Fixed assets	36,000	97,660	144,005
Less: Accumulated depreciation	(21,800)	(62,426)	(99,227)
	£19,800	$48,114	$ 57,798
Bank loan	£ 1,100	$ 2,530	$ 2,530
Payables	5,100	11,730	11,730
Share capital	8,000	24,000	39,632
Retained earnings	5,600	9,854	3,906
	£19,800	$48,114	$ 57,798

Exhibit X

UK Company Ltd.
Statement of Income and Retained Earnings
For the year ended December 31, 1974

	Historical Basis		Price-level Basis
	Sterling	Dollars	1974 $
Sales	£16,300	$37,816	$40,198
Cost of sales:			
Opening inventory	3,300	7,590	8,720
Purchases	10,300	23,896	25,401
Closing inventory	(3,800)	(8,740)	(8,880)
	£ 9,800	$22,746	$25,241
Depreciation	3,600	9,766	14,400
Selling and administrative	800	1,856	1,973
	£14,200	$34,368	$41,614
	£ 2,100	$ 3,448	$ (1,416)
Income taxes	1,000	2,320	2,466
	£ 1,100	$ 1,128	$ (3,882)
Gain on exchange		76	81
General price-level gain			857
Net income	£ 1,100	$ 1,204	$ (2,944)
Retained earnings, beginning of year	4,500	8,650	6,850
Retained earnings, end of year	£ 5,600	$ 9,854	$ 3,906

Converting the 1974 translated balance sheet to a price-level basis

The translated balance sheet in historical Canadian dollars is updated to December 1974 dollars by application of Canadian indices.

(1) The monetary items are receivables, bank loan and payables and require no restatement.

(2) The inventories were acquired during the last three months of 1974 when the average index was say 182. The inventory is therefore updated

$8,740 × 185/182, or 1.016 = $8,880

(3) Fixed assets

	Historical		*Price-level 1974 $*	
	Cost	*Accumulated depreciation*	*Cost*	*Accumulated depreciation*
December 1973	$79,100	$52,660	$108,725	$74,279
Updated to December 1974 dollars at 1.142			$124,164	$84,827
1974 additions	18,560		19,841	
1974 depreciation		9,766		14,400
	$97,660	$62,426	$144,005	$99,227

The addition was made in June 1974 and is converted to December 1974 dollars by application of the conversion factor 185/173, or 1.069.

(4) There have been no transactions in the share capital account since December 1973. The amount in the price-level balance sheet at December 1973 is rolled forward to 1974 dollars.

(5) The balance of retained earnings on a GPL basis flows through from the 1974 GPL income and retained earnings statement.

Translating the 1974 historical income statement

(1) Sales, purchases, selling and administrative and income taxes are translated at the average rate for the year of £1 = $2.32.

(2) The inventories are entered at the same amounts calculated for the balance sheets.

(3) The depreciation is translated at the exchange rates appropriate to the fixed assets and is derived from the analysis of the fixed asset accounts.

(4) The retained earnings figures are entered at the same amounts as in the balance sheets, and the balancing figure is the gain on foreign exchange for the year.

Converting the 1974 translated income statement to a price-level basis

(1) Sales, purchases, selling and administrative expenses and income taxes are assumed to have accrued evenly throughout the year. These items are translated into December 1974 dollars by multiplying by the conversion factor applicable to the average index for the year, i.e. 185/174, or 1.063.
(2) The gain on translation is also assumed to have accrued evenly throughout the year and is converted at the average factor of 1.063.
(3) The inventories and depreciation are entered at the same amounts as calculated for the balance sheet accounts.
(4) The price-level gain or loss is computed by preparing a source and application of monetary items.

	Historical 1973	*Historical 1974*	*Historical 1973 in 1974 $*
Cash	$ 2,300	$ —	$ 2,627
Receivables	3,450	4,140	3,940
Bank loan	—	(2,530)	—
Payables	(7,130)	(11,730)	(8,142)
	$(1,380)	$(10,120)	$(1,575)

		Historical		*Restated 1974 $*
Net monetary items December 31, 1973		$ (1,380)		$(1,575)
Add monetary inflow				
Sales	$37,816		$40,198	
Exchange gain	76		81	
	$37,892		$40,279	
Deduct monetary outflow				
Purchases	$23,896		$25,401	
Selling and administrative	1,856		1,973	
Income taxes	2,320		2,466	
Purchases of assets	18,560		19,841	
	$46,632		$49,681	
Increase in monetary liabilities		8,740		9,402
Restated net monetary liabilities				$(10,977)
Actual net monetary liabilities at December 31, 1974		$(10,120)		(10,120)
General price-level gain				$ 857

The "restate-translate" method

Under this method the statements are prepared on a price-level basis, using the United Kingdom indices, and then translated into Canadian dollars at the closing rate of exchange. The first statement to be prepared on a price-level basis and then translated is the December 1973 balance sheet.

Exhibit Y shows the 1973 sterling balance sheet expressed on a price-level basis in 1973 sterling and translated into 1973 Canadian dollars.

Exhibit Y

UK Company Ltd.
Balance Sheet
December 31, 1973

	Historical Sterling	*Price-level Sterling*	*Price-level 1973 $*
Cash	£ 1,000	£ 1,000	$ 2,300
Receivables	1,500	1,500	3,450
Inventories	3,300	3,333	7,666
Fixed assets	28,000	42,574	97,920
Less: Accumulated depreciation	(18,200)	(28,791)	(66,219)
	£15,600	£19,616	$45,117
Payables	£ 3,100	£ 3,100	$ 7,130
Share capital	8,000	13,064	30,047
Retained earnings	4,500	3,452	7,940
	£15,600	£19,616	$45,117

Converting the 1973 historical balance sheet to a price-level basis

(1) The monetary items are cash, receivables and payables and require no restatement.

(2) The inventories were acquired during the last three months of 1973 when the average index was say 97.

$$£3,300 \times 98/97, \text{ or } 1.010 = £3,333$$

(3) Fixed assets

	Historical			*Price-level 1973 Sterling*	
Year of acquisition	*Cost*	*Acc. dep.*	*Conversion factor*	*Cost*	*Acc. dep.*
1966	£17,000	£13,600	98/60, or 1.633	£27,761	£22,209
1968	6,000	3,600	98/65, or 1.508	9,048	5,429
1972	5,000	1,000	98/85, or 1.153	5,765	1,153
	£28,000	£18,200		£42,574	£28,791

(4) Share capital, issued in 1966

£8,000 × 98/60, or 1.633 = £13,064

Translating the 1973 price-level balance sheet

All amounts are translated at the closing rate of exchange of £1 = $2.30.

Rolling forward the 1973 price-level balance sheet to 1974 price-levels

Exhibit Z shows the 1973 GPL balance sheet in pounds sterling rolled forward to its equivalent in pounds sterling of December 1974 purchasing power by applying the conversion factor 110/98, or 1.122.

* * *

Exhibit AA shows the 1974 sterling balance sheet, expressed on a price-level basis in 1974 sterling and translated into 1974 Canadian dollars.

Exhibit BB shows the 1974 sterling statement of income and retained earnings, similarly expressed on a price-level basis in 1974 sterling and translated into 1974 Canadian dollars.

Exhibit Z

UK Company Ltd.
GPL Balance Sheet
December 31, 1973

	Price-level 1973 Sterling	*Price-level 1974 Sterling*
Cash	£ 1,000	£ 1,122
Receivables	1,500	1,683
Inventories	3,333	3,740
Fixed assets	42,574	47,768
Less: Accumulated depreciation	(28,791)	(32,304)
	£19,616	£22,009
Payables	£ 3,100	£ 3,478
Share capital	13,064	14,658
Retained earnings	3,452	3,873
	£19,616	£22,009

Exhibit AA

UK Company Ltd.
Balance Sheet
December 31, 1974

	Historical Sterling	*Price-level 1974 Sterling*	*Price-level 1974 $*
Receivables	£ 1,800	£ 1,800	$ 4,140
Inventories	3,800	3,834	8,818
Fixed assets	36,000	56,152	129,150
Less: Accumulated depreciation	(21,800)	(37,919)	(87,214)
	£19,800	£23,867	$54,894
Bank loan	£ 1,100	£ 1,100	$ 2,530
Payables	5,100	5,100	11,730
Share capital	8,000	14,658	33,713
Retained earnings	5,600	3,009	6,921
	£19,800	£23,867	$54,894

Exhibit BB

UK Company Ltd.
Statement of Income and Retained Earnings
For the year ended December 31, 1974

	Historical Sterling	*Price-level 1974 Sterling*	*Price-level 1974 $*
Sales	£16,300	£17,245	$39,663
Cost of sales:			
Opening inventory	3,300	3,740	8,602
Purchases	10,300	10,897	25,063
Closing inventory	(3,800)	(3,834)	(8,818)
	£ 9,800	£10,803	$24,847
Depreciation	3,600	5,615	12,914
Selling and administrative	800	846	1,946
	£14,200	£17,264	$39,707
	£ 2,100	£ (19)	$ (44)
Income taxes	1,000	1,058	2,433
	£ 1,100	£ (1,077)	$(2,477)
General price-level gain		213	490
Net income	£ 1,100	£ (864)	$(1,987)
Retained earnings, beginning of year	4,500	3,873	8,908
Retained earnings, end of year	£ 5,600	£ 3,009	$ 6,921

Converting the 1974 historical balance sheet to a price-level basis

(1) The monetary items are receivables, bank loan and payables and require no restatement.

(2) The inventories were acquired during the last three months of 1974 when the average index was say 109.

$$£3,800 \times 110/109, \text{ or } 1.009 = £3,834$$

(3) Fixed assets

	Historical		*Price-level 1974 £*	
	Cost	*Accumulated depreciation*	*Cost*	*Accumulated depreciation*
Balances at December 1973	£28,000	£18,200	£42,574	£28,791
Updated to December 1974 sterling at 1.122			£47,768	£32,304
1974 additions	8,000		8,384	
1974 depreciation		3,600		5,615
	£36,000	£21,800	£56,152	£37,919

The cost of the 1974 additions is converted into December 1974 sterling by the conversion factor 110/105, or 1.048.

(4) Share capital

There have been no transactions in the share capital account; the 1973 sterling price-level amount of £13,064 rolled forward to 1974 pounds sterling of £14,658.

Translating the 1974 price-level balance sheet

All amounts are translated at the closing rate of exchange of £1 = $2.30.

Restating the 1974 income statement

(1) Sales, purchases, selling and administrative expenses and income taxes are restated at the average index for the year, i.e. 110/104, or 1.058.

(2) Inventories and depreciation are entered at the same amounts as calculated for the balance sheets.

(3) The price-level gain or loss is computed by preparing a source and application of monetary items.

	Historical 1973	*Historical 1974*	*Historical 1973 in 1974 Sterling*
Cash	£ 1,000	—	£ 1,122
Receivables	1,500	£ 1,800	1,683
Bank loan		(1,100)	
Payables	(3,100)	(5,100)	(3,478)
	£ (600)	£ (4,400)	£ (673)

		Historical		*Restated 1974 Sterling*
Net monetary items, December 31, 1973		£ (600)		£ (673)
Add monetary inflow				
Sales	£ 16,300		£ 17,245	
Deduct monetary outflow				
Purchases	10,300		10,897	
Selling and administrative	800		846	
Income taxes	1,000		1,058	
Purchases of assets	8,000		8,384	
	£ 20,100		£ 21,185	
Increase in monetary liabilities		3,800		3,940
Restated net monetary liabilities				£ (4,613)
Actual net monetary liabilities at December 31, 1974		£ (4,400)		(4,400)
General price-level gain				£ 213

Translating the 1974 price-level income statement

All items are translated at the closing rate of exchange of £1 = $2.30.

Summary

The different effect of using the translate-restate and the restate-translate methods can be seen in the following GPL statements of UK Company Ltd.

UK Company Ltd.
GPL Balance Sheet at December 31, 1974
(expressed in 1974 Canadian dollars)

	Translate-Restate	*Restate-Translate*
Receivables	$ 4,140	$ 4,140
Inventories	8,880	8,818
Fixed assets	144,005	129,150
Less: Accumulated depreciation	(99,227)	(87,214)
	$ 57,798	$ 54,894
Bank loan	$ 2,530	$ 2,530
Payables	11,730	11,730
Share capital	39,632	33,713
Retained earnings	3,906	6,921
	$ 57,798	$ 54,894

UK Company Ltd.
GPL Statement of Income and Retained Earnings
For the year ended December 31, 1974
(expressed in 1974 Canadian dollars)

	Translate-Restate	*Restate-Translate*
Sales	$40,198	$39,663
Cost of sales	25,241	24,847
Depreciation	14,400	12,914
Selling and administrative	1,973	1,946
	$41,614	$39,707
	$(1,416)	$ (44)
Income taxes	2,466	2,433
	$(3,882)	$(2,477)
Gain on exchange	81	—
General price-level gain	857	490
Net income	$(2,944)	$(1,987)
Retained earnings, beginning of year	6,850	8,908
Retained earnings, end of year	$ 3,906	$ 6,921

Subsidiary located in South America

The following are the statements of RST Company, a subsidiary located in South America, expressed in local currency.

Balance sheet	*December 31*	
	1973	*1974*
Cash	LC 495	LC 528
Receivables	746	554
Inventories	1,651	1,756
Fixed assets (net)	6,012	7,461
	LC 8,904	LC 10,299
Payables	LC 1,534	LC 2,719
Share capital	5,000	5,000
Retained earnings	2,370	2,580
	LC 8,904	LC 10,299

Statement of income and retained earnings	*December 31, 1974*
Sales	LC 7,363
Cost of sales	4,548
Depreciation	2,181
Selling and administrative	369
	7,098
	265
Income taxes	55
Net income	210
Retained earnings, beginning of year	2,370
Retained earnings, end of year	LC 2,580

Assumptions as to indices and exchange rates

	Canada	*Foreign country*	
1966 average	112	200	LC 1.00 = $0.40
1968 average	122	500	$0.30
1972 average	142	900	$0.16
1973 year-end	162	1,300	$0.12
1974 average	174	1,450	$0.10
1974 June	173	1,459	$0.10
1974 year-end	185	1,600	$0.08

The "translate-restate" method

The first statement to be translated and updated is the December 1973 balance sheet.

Exhibit CC shows the 1973 local currency balance sheet, translated into Canadian dollars and expressed on a price-level basis in both 1973 and 1974 dollars.

Exhibit CC

RST Company
Balance Sheet
December 31, 1973

	Historical		*Price-level*	
	Local currency	*Dollars*	*1973 $*	*1974 $*
Cash	LC 495	$ 59	$ 59	$ 67
Receivables	746	90	90	103
Inventories	1,651	198	199	227
Fixed assets	18,181	6,236	8,741	9,982
Less: Accumulated depreciation	(12,169)	(4,488)	(6,372)	(7,277)
	LC 8,904	$2,095	$2,717	$3,102
Payables	LC 1,534	$ 184	$ 184	$ 210
Share capital	5,000	2,000	2,892	3,303
Retained earnings	2,370	(89)	(359)	(411)
	LC 8,904	$2,095	$2,717	$3,102

Translating the 1973 historical balance sheet

(1) Current items such as cash, receivables, inventory and payables are translated at closing rate of exchange of LC 1.00 = $0.12 Canadian.

(2) Fixed assets are converted at rates prevailing at dates of acquisition. Depreciation is at a rate of 10% per annum, straight-line basis.

Year of acquisition	*Local currency*			*Dollars*	
	Cost	*Acc. dep.*	*Exchange rate*	*Cost*	*Acc. dep.*
1966	LC 11,340	LC 9,072	LC 1.00 = $0.40 Can.	$4,536	$3,629
1968	4,322	2,593	LC 1.00 = $0.30 Can.	1,297	778
1972	2,519	504	LC 1.00 = $0.16 Can.	403	81
	LC 18,181	LC 12,169		$6,236	$4,488

(3) The share capital was issued in 1966 and is translated at the rate for that year of LC 1.00 = $0.40 Canadian.

(4) Retained earnings is the balancing figure.

Converting the 1973 translated balance sheet to a price-level basis

The translated balance sheet, expressed in historical Canadian dollars, is updated to December 1973 dollars by application of the Canadian indices.

(1) The monetary items are cash, receivables and payables and require no restatement.

(2) Inventories were acquired during the last three months of 1973 when the average index was say 161. The inventory is therefore updated

$198 × 162/161, or 1.006 = $199

(3) The fixed assets are updated by reference to the indices applicable to their years of acquisition.

Year of acquisition	*Historical*			*Price-level 1973 $*	
	Cost	*Acc. dep.*	*Conversion factor*	*Cost*	*Acc. dep.*
1966	$4,536	$3,629	162/112, or 1.446	$6,559	$5,247
1968	1,297	778	162/122, or 1.328	1,722	1,033
1972	403	81	162/142, or 1.141	460	92
	$6,236	$4,488		$8,741	$6,372

(4) Share capital was issued in 1966.

$2,000 × 162/112, or 1.446 = $2,892

(5) Retained earnings is a balancing figure.

Rolling forward the 1973 price-level balance sheet to 1974 price-levels

The 1973 GPL balance sheet is rolled forward to its equivalent in dollars of December 1974 purchasing power by applying the conversion factor 185/162, or 1.142.

* * *

Exhibit DD shows the 1974 local currency balance sheet translated into Canadian dollars and expressed on a price-level basis in 1974 dollars.

Exhibit EE shows the 1974 local currency statement of income and retained earnings similarly translated into Canadian dollars and expressed on a price-level basis in 1974 dollars.

Exhibit DD

RST Company
Balance Sheet
December 31, 1974

	Historical Basis		*Price-level Basis*
	Local currency	*Dollars*	*1974 $*
Cash	LC 528	$ 42	$ 42
Receivables	554	44	44
Inventories	1,756	140	142
Fixed assets	21,811	6,599	10,370
Less: Accumulated depreciation	(14,350)	(5,148)	(8,314)
	LC 10,299	$1,677	$2,284
Payables	LC 2,719	$ 218	$ 218
Share capital	5,000	2,000	3,303
Retained earnings	2,580	(541)	(1,237)
	LC 10,299	$1,677	$2,284

Exhibit EE

RST Company
Statement of Income and Retained Earnings
For the year ended December 31, 1974

	Historical Basis		Price-level Basis
	Local currency	Dollars	1974 $
Sales	LC 7,363	$ 736	$ 782
Cost of sales:			
Opening inventory	1,651	198	227
Purchases	4,653	465	494
Closing inventory	(1,756)	(140)	(142)
	LC 4,548	$ 523	$ 579
Depreciation	2,181	660	1,037
Selling and administrative	369	37	39
	LC 7,098	$1,220	$ 1,655
	LC 265	$ (484)	$ (873)
Income taxes	55	6	6
	LC 210	$ (490)	$ (879)
Gain on exchange		38	40
General price-level gain			13
Net income	LC 210	$ (452)	$ (826)
Retained earnings, beginning of year	2,370	(89)	(411)
Retained earnings, end of year	LC 2,580	$ (541)	$(1,237)

Translating the 1974 historical balance sheet

(1) Current items such as cash, receivables, inventory and payables are translated at the closing rate of exchange of LC 1.00 = $0.08 Canadian.

(2) Fixed asset and depreciation accounts are translated at historical rates and include the acquisition made in June 1974 and the depreciation provision for 1974.

Year of acquisition	Local currency Cost	Depreciation to 1973	1974	Dollars Cost	Depreciation to 1973	1974
1966	LC 11,340	9,072	1,134	$4,536	3,629	454
1968	4,322	2,593	432	1,297	778	130
1972	2,519	504	252	403	81	40
	18,181	12,169	1,818	6,236	4,488	624
1974	3,630		363	363		36
	LC 21,811	12,169	2,181	$6,599	4,488	660
			12,169			4,488
			LC 14,350			$5,148

(3) Share capital is translated at the rate of exchange prevailing when it was issued in 1966 of LC 1.00 = $0.40 Canadian.

(4) Retained earnings is the balancing figure.

Converting the 1974 translated balance sheet to a price-level basis

(1) The monetary items are cash, receivables and payables and require no restatement.

(2) Inventories were acquired during the last three months of 1974 when the average index was say 182. The inventories are therefore updated

$$\$140 \times 185/182, \text{ or } 1.016 = \$142$$

(3) Fixed assets

	Historical Cost	Historical Accumulated depreciation	Price-level 1974 $ Cost	Price-level 1974 $ Accumulated depreciation
December 1973 balances	$6,236	$4,488	$ 8,741	$6,372
Restated in 1974 dollars			9,982	7,277
Additions in June 1974	363		388	
Depreciation, 1974		660		1,037
	$6,599	$5,148	$10,370	$8,314

The addition was made in June and is converted to December 1974 dollars by application of the conversion factor 185/173, or 1.069.

(4) There have been no transactions in the share capital account since December 1973; the amount in the price-level balance sheet at December 1973 is rolled forward to 1974 dollars.

(5) Retained earnings is the balancing figure.

Translating the 1974 historical income statement

(1) Sales, purchases, selling and administrative and income taxes are translated at the average rate for the year of LC 1.00 = $0.10 Canadian.
(2) Inventories are entered at the same amounts calculated for the balance sheets.
(3) Depreciation is translated at the exchange rates appropriate to the fixed assets and is obtained from the analysis of the fixed asset accounts.
(4) The retained earnings figures are entered at the same amount as in the balance sheets, and the balancing figure is the gain on exchange for the year.

Converting the 1974 translated income statement to a price-level basis

(1) Sales, purchases, selling and administrative and income taxes are assumed to have accrued evenly throughout the year. All are translated into December 1974 dollars by applying the average conversion factor 185/174, or 1.063.
(2) Gain on translation is considered to have accrued evenly throughout the year and is converted at the average factor of 1.063.
(3) Inventories and depreciation are entered at the same amounts as computed for the balance sheet accounts.
(4) The price-level gain or loss is computed by preparing a statement of source and application of monetary items.

	Historical 1973	*Historical 1974*	*Historical 1973 in 1974 $*
Cash	$ 59	$ 42	$ 67
Receivables	90	44	103
Payables	(184)	(218)	(210)
	$ (35)	$(132)	$ (40)

		Historical		*Restated 1974 $*
Net monetary items at December 31, 1973		$ (35)		$ (40)
Add monetary inflow				
Sales	$736		$782	
Exchange gain	38		40	
	$774		$822	
Deduct monetary outflow				
Purchases	$465		$494	
Selling and administrative	37		39	
Income taxes	6		6	
Purchase of assets	363		388	
	$871		$927	
Increase in monetary liabilities		97		105
Restated net monetary liabilities				$(145)
Actual net monetary liabilities at December 31, 1974		$(132)		(132)
General price-level gain				$ 13

The "restate-translate" method

Exhibit FF shows the 1973 local currency balance sheet, expressed on a price-level basis in 1973 local currency and translated into 1973 Canadian dollars.

Exhibit FF

RST Company
Balance Sheet
December 31, 1973

	Historical Local currency	*Price-level Local currency*	*Price-level 1973 Dollars*
Cash	LC 495	LC 495	$ 59
Receivables	746	746	90
Inventories	1,651	1,717	206
Fixed assets	18,181	88,584	10,630
Less: Accumulated depreciation	(12,169)	(66,438)	(7,973)
	LC 8,904	LC 25,104	$ 3,012
Payables	LC 1,534	LC 1,534	$ 184
Share capital	5,000	32,500	3,900
Retained earnings	2,370	(8,930)	(1,072)
	LC 8,904	LC 25,104	$ 3,012

Converting the 1973 historical balance sheet to a price-level basis

(1) Identify all monetary items

(2) Inventories were acquired during the last three months of 1973 when the average index was say 1250

LC 1,651 × 1300/1250, or 1.040 = LC 1,717

(3) Fixed assets

Year of acquisition	*Historical Cost*	*Historical Acc. dep.*	*Conversion factor*	*Price-level 1973 LC Cost*	*Price-level 1973 LC Acc. dep.*
1966	LC 11,340	LC 9,072	1300/200, or 6.500	LC 73,710	LC 58,968
1968	4,322	2,593	1300/500, or 2.600	11,237	6,742
1972	2,519	504	1300/900, or 1.444	3,637	728
	LC 18,181	LC 12,169		LC 88,584	LC 66,438

(4) Share capital was issued in 1966

LC 5,000 × 1300/200, or 6.500 = LC 32,500.

Translating the 1973 price-level balance sheet

All amounts are translated at the closing rate of exchange of LC 1.00 = $0.12 Canadian.

Rolling forward the 1973 price-level balance sheet to 1974 price-levels

Exhibit GG shows the 1973 GPL balance sheet in local currency, rolled forward to its equivalent in local currency of December 1974 purchasing power by applying the conversion factor 1600/1300, or 1.231.

* * *

Exhibit HH shows the 1974 local currency balance sheet expressed on a price-level basis in 1974 local currency and translated into 1974 Canadian dollars.

Exhibit II shows the 1974 local currency statement of income and retained earnings similarly expressed on a price-level basis in 1974 local currency and translated into 1974 Canadian dollars.

Exhibit GG

RST Company
GPL Balance Sheet
December 31, 1973

	Price-level 1973 Local currency	*Price-level 1974 Local currency*
Cash	LC 495	LC 609
Receivables	746	918
Inventories	1,717	2,114
Fixed assets	88,584	109,047
Less: Accumulated depreciation	(66,438)	(81,785)
	LC 25,104	LC 30,903
Payables	LC 1,534	LC 1,888
Share capital	32,500	40,008
Retained earnings	(8,930)	(10,993)
	LC 25,104	LC 30,903

Exhibit HH

RST Company
Balance Sheet
December 31, 1974

	Historical Local currency	*Price-level 1974 Local currency*	*Price-leve 1974 $*
Cash	LC 528	LC 528	$ 42
Receivables	554	554	44
Inventories	1,756	1,874	150
Fixed assets	21,811	113,029	9,042
Less: Accumulated depreciation	(14,350)	(93,088)	(7,447)
	LC 10,299	LC 22,897	$1,831
Payables	LC 2,719	LC 2,719	$ 217
Share capital	5,000	40,008	3,200
Retained earnings	2,580	(19,830)	(1,586)
	LC 10,299	LC 22,897	$1,831

Exhibit II

RST Company
Statement of Income and Retained Earnings
For the year ended December 31, 1974

	Historical Local currency	*Price-level 1974 Local currency*	*Price-level 1974 $*
Sales	LC 7,363	LC 8,121	$ 650
Cost of sales:			
Opening inventory	1,651	2,114	169
Purchases	4,653	5,132	411
Closing inventory	(1,756)	(1,874)	(150)
	LC 4,548	LC 5,372	$ 430
Depreciation	2,181	11,303	904
Selling and administrative	369	407	33
	LC 7,098	LC 17,082	$ 1,367
	LC 265	LC (8,961)	$ (717)
Income taxes	55	61	5
	LC 210	LC (9,022)	$ (722)
General price-level gain		185	15
Net income	LC 210	LC (8,837)	$ (707)
Retained earnings, beginning of year	2,370	(10,993)	(879)
Retained earnings, end of year	LC 2,580	LC (19,830)	$(1,586)

Converting the 1974 historical balance sheet to a price-level basis

(1) Identify all monetary items.
(2) Inventories were acquired during the last three months of 1974 when the average index was say 1500

LC 1,756 × 1600/1500, or 1.067 = LC 1,874.

(3) Fixed assets.

	Historical		*Price-level 1974 LC*	
	Cost	*Acc. dep.*	*Cost*	*Acc. dep.*
Balances at December 31, 1973	LC 18,181	LC 12,169	LC 88,584	LC 66,438
Updated to December 1974 local currency at 1.231			109,047	81,785
Additions in June 1974	3,630		3,982*	
Depreciation, 1974		2,181		11,303
	LC 21,811	LC 14,350	LC 113,029	LC 93,088

*LC 3,630 × 1600/1459, or 1.097 = LC 3,982.

(4) There have been no transactions on share capital account since December 1973; the amount in the 1973 price-level balance sheet is rolled forward to 1974 local currency.

Translating the 1974 price-level balance sheet

All amounts are translated at the closing rate of exchange of LC 1.00 = $0.08 Canadian.

Restating the 1974 income statement

(1) Sales, purchases, selling and administrative expenses and income taxes are requested at the average index for year

1600/1450, or 1.103.

(2) Inventories and depreciation are entered in the same amounts calculated for the balance sheets.
(3) The price-level gain or loss is computed by preparing a statement of source and application of monetary items.

	Historical 1973	*Historical 1974*	*Historical 1973 in 1974 local currency*
Cash	LC 495	LC 528	LC 609
Receivables	746	554	918
Payables	(1,534)	(2,719)	(1,888)
	LC (293)	LC(1,637)	LC (361)

		Historical		*Restated 1974 LC*
Net monetary items December 31, 1973		LC (293)		LC (361)
Add monetary inflow				
Sales	LC 7,363		LC 8,121	
Deduct monetary outflow				
Purchases	4,653		5,132	
Selling and administrative	369		407	
Income taxes	55		61	
Purchases of assets	3,630		3,982	
	LC 8,707		LC 9,582	
Increase in monetary liabilities		1,344		1,461
Restated net monetary liabilities				LC (1,822)
Actual net monetary liabilities at December 31, 1974		LC (1,637)		(1,637)
General price-level gain				LC 185

Translating the 1974 price-level income statement

All amounts are translated at the closing rate of exchange of LC 1.00 = $0.08 Canadian.

Summary

The different effect of using the translate-restate and the restate-translate methods can be seen in the following GPL statements of RST Company.

RST Company
GPL Balance Sheet at December 31, 1974
(expressed in 1974 Canadian dollars)

	Translate-Restate	*Restate-Translate*
Cash	$ 42	$ 42
Receivables	44	44
Inventories	142	150
Fixed assets	10,370	9,042
Less: Accumulated depreciation	(8,314)	(7,447)
	$ 2,284	$1,831
Payables	$ 218	$ 217
Share capital	3,303	3,200
Retained earnings	(1,237)	(1,586)
	$ 2,284	$1,831

RST Company
GPL Statement of Income and Retained Earnings
For the year ended December 31, 1974
(expressed in 1974 Canadian dollars)

	Translate-Restate	*Restate-Translate*
Sales	$ 782	$ 650
Cost of sales	579	430
Depreciation	1,037	904
Selling and administrative	39	33
	$ 1,655	$ 1,367
	$ (873)	$ (717)
Income taxes	6	5
	$ (879)	$ (722)
Gain on exchange	40	
General price-level gain	13	15
Net income	$ (826)	$ (707)
Retained earnings, beginning of year	(411)	(879)
Retained earnings, end of year	$(1,237)	$(1,586)

12

Presentation of GPL Statements in Annual Reports

GPL financial statements are intended as supplementary statements. Conventional historical cost statements are still required for statutory, taxation and many other legal purposes. Price-level statements would complement the historical cost statements but are not intended to replace them.

While GPL accounting is still relatively new, the amount of price-level information included in published annual reports can be expected to vary from, on the one hand, an indication of or passing reference to the approximate effect of inflation on the results of operations to, on the other hand, the provision of complete GPL financial statements as supplementary information. Within these two extremes, a range of other possibilities exists.

1. The figure for net income and/or earnings per share computed on the price-level basis.
2. Selected information computed on the price-level basis, such as sales, total assets, net income and earnings per share.
3. A condensed GPL balance sheet and income statement on the price-level basis, with or without explanatory notes.
4. A complete GPL balance sheet and income statement showing each item in the historical cost statements at the price-level adjusted amount, with or without explanatory notes.

In each case the GPL details may be presented in the annual report elsewhere than in the historical financial statements (for example, in a directors' report) or in such a way that they appear to be part of the historical financial statements. Nevertheless, in the latter case, they remain supplementary information and do not become part of the historical financial statements.

Disclosing only a single figure of net income or earnings per share on the price-level basis does not inform the shareholder of the basis used to arrive at either figure; because GPL accounting is still largely in an experimental stage and differences in practice are likely to continue for some time, an indication of the basis used is considered essential if the shareholder is to be properly informed. Furthermore, the point must again be emphasized that GPL accounting introduces estimates and approximations which extend the tolerances already inherent in historical financial statements. There is thus a potential danger in stating a single GPL figure, whether it is net income or earnings per share, without giving recognition to this characteristic of GPL accounting.

On the other hand, providing complete GPL financial statements showing the restated amount of each item may provide more detail than is necessary in most cases. It is unlikely that restatement of every item in the historical financial statements would prove useful to a shareholder and in fact the extra detail might tend to confuse rather than enlighten. A compromise between the extremes of inadequate and exaggerated disclosure should be sought.

Supplementary GPL information that it would generally be reasonable and useful to include in annual reports might include

(a) a comparative condensed balance sheet and income statement showing price-level and historical amounts in parallel columns,
(b) an explanation of the basis used in preparing the price-level statements, including identification of the index used,
(c) an explanation that the statements do not represent current values, and
(d) a reconciliation of the net income figure shown in the price-level accounts with that shown in the historical cost accounts.

If the company normally publishes ratios based on the historical cost amounts, the same ratios based on the GPL amounts might be published, subject to the concern already expressed about undue precision being attributed to single GPL figures such as restated earnings per share.

As mentioned earlier (see page 11), a statement of changes in financial position on a price-level basis serves no particular purpose and its inclusion in GPL statements is therefore not recommended.

Ten-year summaries

The ten-year summaries which many companies now include in the annual reports provide useful information on the progress of the business. If this information were presented on a price-level basis, with every figure expressed in currency units of the same value, the true rate of progress or otherwise would be clearly evident. The work of restating these summaries on a price-level basis may be unduly onerous, and in practice they would more probably be built up over future years as the price-level information is accumulated. It is perfectly feasible however, to restate, say, the sales figures over the last ten years on the basis of dollars of current purchasing power.

International corporations

Some multinational corporations publish their statements in two or more languages or currencies. Where statements are presented in a currency different from the domestic currency of the company, they normally represent secondary statements, i.e. statements in addition to the primary statements of the company expressed in its domestic currency. In such cases they are merely a translation of the domestic currency statements and any foreign currency price-level statements would also be merely a translation of the domestic currency price-level statements.

Some companies have adopted the practice of presenting their primary statutory financial statements in a foreign currency; for example, a number of companies in Canada publish their financial statements in United States dollars rather than in Canadian dollars because of the extent of their operations in the United States. With regard to these companies, the question arises which index should be used in the preparation of GPL statements. Should it be a Canadian general price-level index as the company is Canadian? Or should it be a United States general price-level index as the currency is the United States dollar?

The purpose of price-level accounting is to measure the effects of the change in the purchasing power of currency on the financial statements during the period covered by those financial statements. In the case of a Canadian company preparing its statements in United States dollars the use of a Canadian general price-level index would not achieve this purpose. The Canadian index would be based on the purchasing power level of the Canadian dollar, but this would be of no relevance to financial statements expressed in a different currency. The only index that has relevance to statements expressed in United States currency is a United States general price-level index.

Illustration of presentation in annual report

Using the consolidated financial statements of ABC Company prepared in Chapter 9, the following is an example of how supplementary price-level information might be presented in a condensed form to shareholders.

ABC Company
Summarized Consolidated Balance Sheet
December 31, 1974
(including supplementary information on a general price-level basis)

	Historical		*Price-level basis*	
	1974	*1973*	*1974*	*1973*
Current assets	$172,832	xxx	$172,893	xxx
Investments	13,110	xxx	16,802	xxx
Fixed assets	257,537	xxx	372,007	xxx
Other assets	413	xxx	709	xxx
Goodwill	216	xxx	289	xxx
	$444,108	xxx	$562,700	xxx
Current liabilities	$ 63,100	xxx	$ 63,100	xxx
Long-term debt	52,180	xxx	49,644	xxx
Deferred income taxes	49,680	xxx	49,680	xxx
Minority interest	3,441	xxx	4,722	xxx
Shareholders' equity	275,707	xxx	395,554	xxx
	$444,108	xxx	$562,700	xxx

ABC Company
Summarized Consolidated Statement of Income and Retained Earnings for the year ended December 31, 1974
(including supplementary information on a general price-level basis)

	Historical		*Price-level basis*	
	1974	*1973*	*1974*	*1973*
Revenues	$436,185	xxx	$462,403	xxx
Expenses	387,404	xxx	435,656	xxx
	48,781	xxx	26,747	xxx
Income taxes	24,778	xxx	26,339	xxx
	24,003	xxx	408	xxx
Equity in earnings of associated company	550	xxx	313	xxx
	24,553	xxx	721	xxx
Price-level adjustments —				
General price-level gain	—	—	8,431	xxx
Foreign currency debt	—	—	4,135	xxx
Reduction of investments to market value	—	—	(1,285)	xxx
			11,281	xxx
	24,553	xxx	12,002	xxx
Minority interest	248	xxx	32	xxx
Net income	24,305	xxx	11,970	xxx
Retained earnings	181,665	xxx	224,856	xxx
	205,970	xxx	236,826	xxx
Dividends	16,113	xxx	17,238	xxx
Retained earnings	$189,857	xxx	$219,588	xxx
Earnings per share	$0.39		$0.18(1)	

(1) *This calculation does not reflect any adjustment in respect of the price-level gain on preferred shares which has been taken direct to shareholders' equity. The FASB exposure draft suggests that such price-level gains should enter into the calculation of net income per common share.*

Notes to the supplementary price-level adjusted statement

1. The amounts in the price-level columns have been arrived at by converting the corresponding figures in the historical columns by reference to changes in the (*name of index*) between

the dates of the original transactions and December 31, 1974. The price-level amounts are measured in dollars of December 31, 1974 purchasing power. The index at December 31, 1974 was 185 and at December 31, 1973 was 162. Both indices are based on 1961 = 100.

2. Restatement of financial statements for price-level changes is essentially an extension of historical cost accounting. The basis for each item reported is its historical cost in terms of its current purchasing power. The characteristics of GPL accounting are such that absolute precision should not be attributed to the amounts.

   Price-level restatements are not intended to reflect replacement costs, reproduction costs or resale prices of assets, nor the current discounted equivalent (present value) of long-term receivables or debts.

3. The following is a reconciliation between net income on the historical cost basis and net income on the price-level basis.

Net income on the historical basis	$24,305
Price-level adjustments	
Additional charge based on restating the cost of inventories at the beginning and end of the year in dollars of current purchasing power, thus taking the inflationary gain out of the profit on the sale of inventories	(16,076)
Additional depreciation based on cost of fixed assets measured in terms of current purchasing power	(9,113)
General price-level gain in purchasing power resulting from the effects of inflation on net monetary liabilities	8,431
General price-level gain on foreign currency debentures	4,135
Increase in sales, purchases and other items	1,463
Provisions to reduce investments to market value	(1,175)
Net income on the price-level basis	$11,970

Note 1 The items which are composed of several amounts in the income statement are analyzed at the end of these specimen notes to the financial statements.

2 When this information is presented on a comparative basis an additional price-level adjustment is needed to update the historical net income. This also is discussed more fully at the end of the notes.

4. The general price-level gain includes amounts arising on long-term debt and deferred income taxes; these amounted to

$65,329 at December 1973. This amount is equivalent to $74,605 measured in terms of dollars at December 1974 value. As these items are considered to be monetary, i.e. fixed in money terms, they have declined in real terms from $74,605 to $65,329 during the year. This reduction of $9,276 in the company's obligations in terms of current purchasing power is taken into account in arriving at the gain on net monetary liabilities of $8,431. It must be emphasized that while this is a gain arising from changes in the purchasing power of money it is not represented by cash.

* * *

The following shows how two amounts in the reconciliation of historical and GPL net income were arrived at; other amounts in the reconciliation are taken direct from the consolidated income statement of ABC Company. (See page 154.)

	Historical	*Price-level*	*Increase*
Cost of sales	$263,223	$295,722	$ 32,499
Less: Purchases			
Parent	258,000	274,254	
Subsidiary	4,563	4,850	
	$262,563	$279,104	
Intercompany elimination	1,750	1,868	
	$260,813	$277,236	16,423
Inventories	$ 2,410	$ 18,486	$ 16,076

Increase in sales, purchases and other items			
Revenue	$436,185	$462,403	$ 26,218
Purchases (as above)	260,813	277,236	16,423
Selling and administrative	101,190	107,661	6,471
Interest	4,221	4,500	279
Income taxes	24,778	26,339	1,561
			$ 24,734
			$ 1,484
Associated company	550	313	237
			$ 1,247
Minority interest	248	32	216
			$ 1,463

The condensed financial statements shown in this illustration do not include comparative figures as these were not developed for this particular example. When the 1975 statements are presented, the 1974 price-level statements will be rolled forward to dollar values at December 1975 and presented as the comparative statements. For example, the index assumed in this illustration at December 1974 was 185; if the index at December 1975 is 204, the 1974 statements will be rolled forward by applying the index 204/185, or 1.103.

As referred to earlier, when presenting a reconciliation in comparative form of net income on the price-level basis with historical net income, it becomes necessary to include an additional price-level adjustment to update historical net income of the previous year in terms of purchasing power at the end of the current year. This separate adjustment arises because each of the reconciling items is derived from the GPL restatement of individual items or groups of items which do not directly affect the previous year's historical net income. Thus in reproducing the above reconciliation in comparative form in 1975 and assuming as before a conversion factor of 1.103, the additional price-level adjustment would appear as

Adjustment to restate 1974 historical net income in terms of 1975 dollars	$2,503*

*($24,305 × 1.103) — $24,305.

Index